CAREST THOU NOT THAT I PERISH?

In the Midst of the Storm

Lydia P. Ford

The Gap Closer™

A Gap Closer™ Publication
WINDSOR, CONNECTICUT

CAREST THOU NOT THAT I PERISH?

In the Midst of the Storm

Cover Photography: **Dr. Angela D. Massey**
Edited by **Dr. Angela D. Massey**

A Gap Closer ™ Publication
A Division of Life On Purpose Publishing
Windsor, Connecticut

Carest Thou Not That I Perish?: In the Midst of the Storm
ISBN: 978-0-9961908-31

In loving memory of my husband,
Deacon Thomas Perry Ford
(1951–2011)

and

His oldest sister: Katherine Jane Turpin-Ford
(1953–2011)

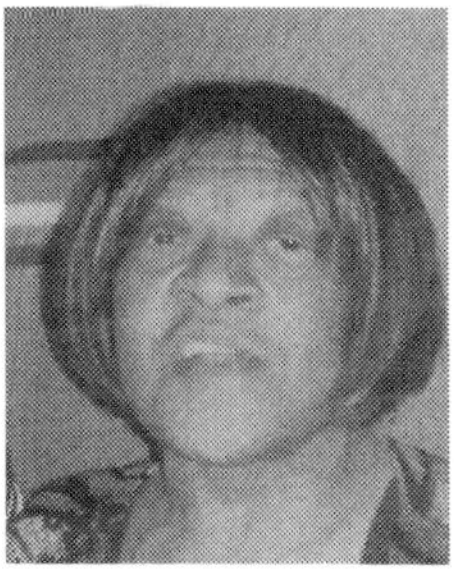

ACKNOWLEDGEMENTS

A special thanks to my mother and sister for keeping me company for many days after my husband died. I also thank my brother-in-law Kevin Ford and sister-in-law, Reverend Darlene Wilson and the rest of the Ford family for their continued love and support. I continue to appreciate and thank family members, prayer partners, members and friends from Hopewell Baptist Church and the Rawson School Prayer Band for their support, love, and encouragement

Cookie Green, thank you for braving the storm and trucking through all of that snow, so that we could do the program for Tom's home-going service.

A special shout out to my son Trevor James Ford and my new daughter-in-law Allyson Davis Ford. You and Ally had the courage and strength to carry on with your wedding plans after your dad's death. People were amazed and surprised at the strength and faith of the Ford Family. You guys had a beautiful wedding on November 19, 2011.

DEDICATION

I dedicate this book to my late husband, Deacon Thomas P. Ford and my son, Trevor James Ford. Tom was my husband for 37 years. I thank God for the gift that he allowed me to know and love for over 40 years. Words cannot express the void that was left after his sudden passing. In my wildest dreams I could not have imagined that my husband would not be present to rejoice with me at the releasing of my first book, *Don't Forget to Say Your Prayers*.

What a shock it was when my husband and I learned of his terminal illness. It came from out of nowhere and literally took my breath away. I was numb after hearing the news. It had been almost a year since the death of our only daughter Danielle, who passed on October 28, 2010. Ironically, Tom passed on October 28, 2011 a year later.

When something tragic like this happens consecutively, you wonder if you will be able to survive. I thank God for the strength that He gave me to persevere through this tumultuous storm.

My husband was such an awesome man. He had a kind and generous spirit. Every morning when he woke up he had a great attitude. He was full of smiles and songs. My granddaughter awakens with that same spirit and attitude like her Papa every day.

Tom treated everyone with respect. He never looked down on anyone. He was a dedicated social worker and loved working with families. He loved his church, family, and was faithful to the Deacons Ministry. He had the gift of evangelism and enjoyed talking to people in the malls, at the grocery stores, on the street, etc. He always took the opportunity to share Jesus Christ with those whom he came in touch with. If a stranger begged him for money on the street, he would tell them," I will give this money to you but I want to share something with you before I give it to you. And, by the way, this is God's money not mine, so be careful how you use it."

Tom loved God and enjoyed the worship experience. He led praise and worship many times. He had a saying that went like this: "Ain't no party like a Holy Ghost party, because a Holy Ghost party don't stop." Tom always exhorted the people to praise the Lord while they had a chance. He was full of joy in the Lord. Hopewell Baptist Church will not be the same without him.

It was awesome to look around at the funeral and see the sea of faces that were in the audience. There were so many people present on that day, but I did not have the presence of mind to fathom or take it all in. I was still pretty numb and tried to keep a stiff upper lip and hold it together. I couldn't believe that this was happening to me again.

I chose not to go into too many details with others regarding Tom's short illness. I just told people to pray for his healing and swift recovery. Suffice it to say that it was devastating news to realize that he would not be coming home again. We really didn't get to say our goodbyes because things progressed so quickly. Tom entered into the hospital on October 3rd. We celebrated our 37th wedding anniversary on October 5th. He turned 60 on the 21st of October and died on the 28th. What a whirlwind of a month!

On his memorial marker at the bottom, I had engraved these words: "Let the party begin." Anyone who happens to go to his grave site would hopefully remember the rest of the saying.

It is important that I say just a note about my son Trevor. He keeps asking me why I didn't write a page about him, so this is what I would like to say to him in this book.

Trevor, I am very proud of you. You have been through quite a lot in your young life. Losing your paternal grandparents, great-grandmother Sylvia, sister and father in the span of a few years has been challenging and difficult for you.

Handling death and dying is not something we expect our children to be equipped to do. Older folks—both the saved and the unsaved—have a difficult time dealing with sickness and death, too. Death and dying is a subject that we would rather eliminate from our psyche.

However, at each home-going service, you chose to articulate the positive attributes that each family member possessed; you reminded, remembered and shared with others the impact that each one had on your life and theirs as well. At our most critical moment you had the discipline and self-control needed to make the right decision for our family. Thank you for your love, care, and support during such a difficult time.

Moreover, I thank my awesome granddaughter Jayla Marie for keeping alive the memory of her mother, Danielle Marie and her Papa, Thomas Ford. She has her mother's quick wit, energy, intelligence, love of music, and passion. She has her Papa's smile, sensitive heart, and love for life. She is my joy and my crown. Jayla is a truly anointed vessel that will be used mightily in the Kingdom of God.

FOREWORD

If you have been under attack by the enemy or by your own thoughts, then this book is for you! If you have experienced suffering of *any* kind and you thought that you would lose your mind, then this book is for you!

If you have unknowingly or knowingly allowed sin to oppress you and overtake you through unforgiveness, hate or bitterness perhaps caused by childhood trauma or abuse, then this book is for you! If you are tired of being held bondage by the dead weights that have held you captive during your young adult or adult life, then this book is for you!

You will have the opportunity to face the truth of your brokenness and allow your damaged heart to begin to heal as you read through this powerful book written by and told through the lens of Pastor Lydia P. Ford.

This book will encourage you to firmly trust God as you continue to stand "*in the midst of the storm*" all while allowing God to heal and restore you unto Him.

I pray that as you take the opportunity to read this compelling book that you will truly open up your heart to allow the Holy Spirit to do the work that God has predestined.

I pray that you will relinquish the unfruitful matters of your heart over to our Lord and Savior, Jesus Christ so that you can walk fully in the anointing that God has entrusted you with.

Be Healed in Jesus' Name!

His Servant unto Death,

Minister Syrette W. Green, LMSW
Wellsprings Counseling Services, LLC
West Hartford, Connecticut

CONTENTS

INTRODUCTION

Nothing builds and develops our character like handling losses or going through the death experience. You can be certain that life as you have previously known it will never be the same again. When you lose a father, mother, husband, child, job, health, or reputation, you are left with some options:

- You can decide that life is not worth living anymore and sink into depression and despair.
- You can believe that the last terrible event that Satan perpetrated against you was the fatal blow, and *this thing* was the catalyst that proves he has the power to destroy your life.
- You can get up, raise your hands to the Lord and decree and declare: "I'm coming out of this; I am more than a conqueror through Christ Jesus!"

After having dealt with and gone through the trauma of losing my daughter, I could have lost my mind and given up all hope of realizing my dreams and aspirations. Instead, I put all of my energies into writing my first book, *Don't Forget to Say Your Prayers*. It is easy to become stagnant and be in limbo as to what to do next because we can become lost between two worlds. That is, the world that we once knew with our loved ones—this world represents our past. Then there is the world we have to decide to live in—this world represents our undetermined future. This heaviness looms over us like the dark ominous clouds before a thunder storm.

Without a foundation, a road map, a GPS system to guide us when we are in a strange land, we can become like the children of Israel who were aghast when they found themselves in Babylonian captivity. When they came to themselves they uttered these words:

> *"By the rivers of Babylon, there we sat down, yea, we wept, when we remembered Zion. We hanged our harps upon the willows in the midst thereof. For they that carried us away captive required of us a song. And they that wasted us required of us mirth, saying, Sing us one of the songs of Zion. How shall we sing the Lord's song in a strange land?" (Psalm 137:1–4 KJV)*

In other words, "How do you expect us to perform for you as if this devastation hasn't meant anything to us? This is not business as usual! Something has happened here. Our lives will never be the same again. You—the enemy—have invaded our lives and taken from us the dearest and best gifts. You have taken us captive and thrown us into a place of unfamiliarity and uncertainty." And on a more personal note: "I don't even know who I am anymore. Don't expect me to get over this anytime soon. Don't expect me to go on as if my life hasn't been shattered into pieces. Don't expect me to be in church Sunday shouting and praising the Lord. I am troubled in my spirit and I have an ache in my heart that I have never experienced before. When I remember all that you have done to me I get mad as hell! Do not ask me to sing any songs just so you'll feel better or feel as though you've won."

When you are in a strange place, a strange land, it is easy to become overwhelmed. Our faith tells us that God will and can ultimately work every situation out for our good. (Romans 8:28). God is able to turn our mourning into dancing. (Psalm 30:11). But until then, in those in-between places or times, what do we do? How do we manage our emotions? How do we balance the spiritual with the practical application of our well-being, so that we can get the maximum healing and benefit from these troubling times?

When Israel's spiritual leader, Moses, was taken from them the nation experienced tremendous loss. The people were in such anguish and remorse. The Bible says that Israel wept for 30 days in the plains of Moab. (Deuteronomy 34:8). God allowed them to weep and grieve for their spiritual father. Likewise, in the New Testament Book of John, we have a story that tells us what happened when Jesus got to Lazarus' tomb and saw Mary, Martha, the women, and others weeping at their brother's grave side, The Bible says that, "Jesus wept." (John 11:35).

This information can be helpful to believers because it shows us in Scripture that grieving is a natural and necessary process. If Jesus—our Lord and Savior, God himself—cried, what makes us think that we shouldn't? In Moses's case, God's response wasn't, "You all should not be crying like that! I'm God, and I'm your real spiritual father; forget about Moses. After all, I am the one who brought you over the Red Sea. I am the one who fed you manna from heaven. I am the one who hewed out water from the rock. You were just following instructions." No, not so, God didn't say, "Get over it and toughen up! You just need to have more faith; you just need to trust Me!"

Guess what my sister and my brother? When you start to hear a lot of religious mumble-jumble, get away as quickly as possible from those kinds of people! When counsel sounds religious and seems out of touch with reality, it doesn't come from God. God doesn't expect us to be robots. He doesn't require us to be super-spiritual and out of balance. How can we deny our grief and pretend that it doesn't hurt or exist? No, God gives us time to grieve, weep, and mourn. The process back to normalcy, to regaining our joy, peace, laughter and dance *will* take time. The Word says: "To everything there is a season, and a time to every purpose under the heaven. A time to weep, and a time to mourn, and a time to dance;" (Ecclesiastes 3: 1, 4) KJV.

God is a God of mercy and compassion. He allowed the nation of Israel to take off 30 days from work to feel, think, and deal with their grief and situation. We have to remember that God cares deeply for us. He has a collection in heaven of every tear we have shed. Our tears are what God uses to process us and get us through our losses and on to our healing.

The process God ultimately prepares for us will produce healing and enable us to get back into life. If we allow ourselves the right to weep, there will be a time to laugh, play and enjoy life again. One thing is for sure—we will either complete our grief or repeat our grief. Once we have completed it we will be left with memories and visual mind pictures that do not haunt us or make us feel bad, rather they will be sweet memories that make us smile, chuckle, laugh out loud, or leave us with a tender warm spot in our hearts.

God the Father, Son, and the precious Holy Spirit continues to work with me, in me, and through me to manifest healing in my mind, body, and spirit. After the consecutive deaths of Danielle and Tom, I was left in a fog. I was speechless and I was moving and doing things almost mechanically. Tom's death occurred the day before Storm Alfred arrived on the East Coast and primarily in Connecticut. There was no time to prepare for the storm. I had been running back and forth to the hospital for days. I didn't have any time; I didn't even have a time out! The forecast didn't prepare us for the tremendous loss and damage that would remain for weeks and weeks after the storm ceased. Neither did it prepare me for the plethora of challenges I would face in order to prepare for the funeral. Power outages, trees down, traffic signals out of order, living arrangement changes, the accident that totaled my car the day before the funeral, family arriving from out of town that needed housing, etc. all of these issues demanded time, clear thinking and action to resolve them—in the midst of sorrow and grief.

I praise God for keeping me through all of those rough days. It has been a little over four years now since Tom has been gone. I am grateful and have the testimony that I don't look like all that I have been through. This tragic event has not left me immobilized.

To the contrary, this trial has changed the entire scope and landscape of my life. It has brought about changes that I may have not been strong enough and ready to fulfill prior to Tom's death. Presently, I am in the founding pastor of Don't Forget To Say Your Prayers International Worship Center located in Windsor, Connecticut. The Lord allowed me to make several transitions in my ministry. I never would have thought in my wildest dreams that I would leave the church I was a member of and served in for 28 years to pastor my own congregation. Romans 8:28 states, "God works everything for our good." In the midst of the greatest upheaval in my life God was preparing me to go to my next level in ministry.

Additionally, God has opened the door to pursue a career as an author. There are other opportunities awaiting me because I made a decision to live and not die! I decided that since the Lord awakened the sleeping giant within me, I must go headlong into it and seek the hidden treasures in dark places. This discovery, of course, means that I have to get out of my comfort zone. If I remain in my comfort zone, I can expect the same things to exist year after year. But to get something that I have never had before, I must be willing to do something new and different. That is why it is imperative that we ask God, "What is my purpose? What is it that I was created to do with the least amount of energy and frustration?"

God wants us to grow in our trials and learn from them. Life goes on. I have my family to consider and three beautiful granddaughters. It is important to me that I finish the divinely appointed work the Lord has asked me to do. The blessing, I should say the over-flowing blessings, will not be released until I am doing the Kingdom assignment that He has ordained me to do. My obedience will set me up to reap the benefits on earth that He has promised me.

I want to able to say what the Apostle Paul said when he came to the end of his life: "For I am now ready to be offered, and the time of my departure is at hand. I have fought a good fight, I have finished my course, I have kept the faith." (2 Timothy 4:6–7).

I pray this book will encourage and inspire you to continue to do the work that the Lord has assigned and purposed for you to do. For those that may or may not have a personal relationship with God, I pray that you will begin to see the reality of needing a God that can comfort you and bring you triumphantly through every burden and obstacle in your life. All God wants is His creations to come, dine and fellowship with Him through the dialog of prayer, which is merely a conversation with Him. It is through this relationship that intimacy evolves. When you abandon all to God and come to Him with no hidden agenda—when you worship, praise, and glorify Him, He will turn His face toward you and nudge, tug, jostle and love on you, and make Himself known to you in a very real way. God never forces Himself on anybody. But you can be sure that His desire is to have a loving continued relationship with you.

I pray that somehow through the reading of this book, you will see and feel my heart, and know why I have decided to make Jesus my first choice and not my last chance. He is the source of my strength. He is the one that restores everything that the enemy has stolen from me. He is the ruler, keeper and sustainer of all life. If you let Him, He will turn the hearts of kings, queens and people of power and influence in your direction, so that you can accomplish the great things that He says you can do. And as always, I remind you as I did with my inaugural book of the same title, *Don't Forget to Say Your Prayers*.

Pastor Lydia P. Ford
Bloomfield, Connecticut

CHAPTER ONE

I CRIED MY LAST TEAR

Mary, Mary the sister Gospel artists, recorded a song entitled *Yesterday*. This song summed up every emotion of grief and despair that encroached upon my life before, during, and after the death of my daughter, Danielle.

This song reminded me that I had to get myself together. I had spent time praying and crying before, during, and after Danie died. Life could not continue on this way. After her death, I was completely devastated and in shock that God did not answer my prayers for healing. I was upset, frustrated and angry with God. I knew I was wrong to feel this way, so I constantly asked Him to remove the bitterness and anger from my heart. I knew that God was sovereign and that He could do whatever He wanted to do, when He wanted, and how He wanted to do it. She was His child. He loved her before I ever knew her. I needed to find comfort in knowing that she was safe in God's arms and that sickness and constant pain would no longer ravage her frail body.

One day while visiting my mom in South Carolina, I was washing up in her bathroom. I looked into the mirror and saw my face. It was an ugly reminder of the effect that too much grief, crying and suffering can have on your face, particularly above your eyelids, under your eyes, and around your mouth. Everything looked dark and there were lines everywhere. I was a little embarrassed and ashamed that I had let myself get this way. I had conditioned myself, I thought, as an intercessor to keep the faith and have a more positive outlook on life. I knew of the hope we have in Christ after we make our transition from earth to glory. The Bible says the life we will experience in heaven with Christ is not to be compared to our former life here on earth.

The fact was, I had a problem and I was not casting all my cares on Him, so that He would give me the grace to make it through this awful experience. Determined to fix me and the situation, I decided to write about what I was going through. The result of my grappling with this pain culminated in the writing of my first book.

The book was the catharsis that helped to ease some of the pain, anxiety, frustration, and dry some tears of a nightly regime to which I had grown accustomed. I started to believe that I could not take Danie's death personally.

God allowed me to go through this experience so that I could explain the process, not the purpose. He wanted me to encourage others to continue to pray, trust God, and hold on to their faith when sickness, death and dying disrupts the family structure.

The book was pretty much completed during the summer and fall of 2011. There were a few obstacles and stumbling blocks the enemy put in the way to delay the publication of the book. The book went through revisions and edits due to grammatical errors. Putting my best foot forward in this first effort as an author was the goal. My friend Angela helped with some of the editing and formatting, which was a blessing. By late summer around September things were moving along quite well. My husband was getting excited about the prospects of having an author for a wife. And then. . .*the storm came*! My husband started complaining about having pain in his shoulder and back. Blood work showed that his platelets were below normal but not within the danger level that would arouse suspicion of a blood disorder or cancer scare. Tom was under doctor's care for diabetes control, weight gain, and high blood pressure. He was seeing a number of doctors for one thing or another. However, he started complaining about shortness of breath. It was difficult for him to walk six feet without having to sit down. During the summer months both of us decided to work on our health issues. We began walking in the mornings. We were walking up to two and a half miles at least three to four times a week. When the issue of shortness of breath came up, I was surprised because he had not shown any problems with breathing throughout the summer and into September.

Tom made an appointment with his internist who decided to prescribe an antibiotic for him. He was also treated for water retention in the chest and lung area. Tom remained on the antibiotic for about ten days without relief. We went back to the doctor. Upon his examination, he immediately sent him for an X-ray and an MRI. The X-ray results were read by the technician and relayed to the doctor. We went back to the physician who told us to get to the hospital right away. All of this drama happened on the same day.

We entered Saint Francis Hospital's Emergency Department, and they immediately put Tom on a breathing machine. Before evening, he was admitted and placed in a hospital room. I will not take the time to reveal the private details of the procedures and tests that Tom had to endure. Suffice it to say, when all was said and done Tom was diagnosed with stage four lung cancer. There was no recommended treatment—no chemo, no radiation—no chance of survival. The news hit us like a ton of bricks.

Day after day I watched Tom whose breathing was aided by a machine and thought to myself, "This cannot be happening again. Where is God? Why is He allowing the devil to ruin our lives? God, are you sleeping? Don't you care that we are still recovering from Danie's death?" My spirit man went into action, "Oh no, devil! You can't do this! The blood of Jesus is against you!" The doctor was all too anxious to show me the X-rays and the lesions that were in both lungs. I looked at them too, but there was still something inside of me that said, *"But with God all things are possible."* My faith in God kicked in again.

There is something about a true believer, that when the chips are down they will say like Job said (paraphrased): "All my appointed time I am going to wait on the Lord." God has the last word regardless to the stage of any disease. There is always hope in the heart of a believer who trust in God.

But what do you do when God tells you, "Your loved one is going to leave you, but I will not let him suffer as long as Danielle did." What do you do then? I heard Him tell me that one morning when I was in the shower. All I could do was weep and try to prepare myself for the next few days ahead.

I was like a zombie. The first week or so, I called in sick and spent hours at the hospital. The next week, I took off time, and tried to work a day here or there. The third week, I did the same thing. I could not bear the thought of watching my husband die from lung cancer and he didn't even smoke! I did not understand what happened. I thought I was through crying for a while. I was beginning to see hope. I was beginning to see my ministry rising from the grave and resurrecting. I had so much to offer. I would write, do workshops and seminars about bereavement and grief. "I am about to make a comeback," I thought to myself.

But then the storm came! Early one morning while on my way to work for a half day, I got a call from the hospital. They told me that Tom had gone into cardiac arrest and they had resuscitated him per our DNR request. They told me that his heart had stopped beating for seven or more minutes and that he probably had sustained brain damage. Essentially, he was brain dead and the only thing keeping him alive was the machine.

When I arrived at ICU and walked into the room, my heart sank. Flashbacks of seeing my daughter in ICU for the last time erupted in my soul like an earthquake. I called out to Tom, but he could not answer. His eyes were opened, but he did not follow me as I moved my finger from left to right. I felt hopeless; I lacked any words to say to anyone. The doctors were pressuring me to make a decision. They had only given him days or a few weeks to live anyway. But they did not know it was October 28th, the day that Danielle passed a year before. They did not know the anguish playing in my mind—first, knowing that our daughter went home to be with the Lord on that very same day—now, my husband as well. How could I make a decision to have the nurses disconnect the machine on this very same day?

I began to remind God that today was the day that Danielle died. "How can you expect me to let Tom go on the same day? God, that's asking way too much!" I was overcome with doubts and fears! I thank God for my son, Pastor, and a few friends that were present to lend their support at this difficult time. My son spoke up courageously and said, "Mom, Dad would not want to be kept alive by a machine. You have to let him go so he and Danie can be together." That was the hardest decision I have ever made in my life. The nurses prepared me and told me what I could expect. They asked me if I wanted to be in the room when they removed the breathing tube. I told them, "No." They said they would come and get me immediately after it was removed. I went to the bathroom and right after that a nurse came and brought me back into the room. I was just in time. Tom's heart was just about to give out. I held his hand and kissed him. The nurse said it seemed like he waited for me to return. He took two short breaths and then he was gone. I looked at the monitor and all I saw was a flat line.

He was gone from this earth, and was now dwelling in the presence of his Lord. If I thought I had cried my last tear for a while, I was wrong. Tears rolled down my face like a flood. I could not believe this was happening again. I was numb. I had to go home to prepare for a home-going service for my husband. The month of October was filled with tender moments, times of celebrating our anniversary, Trevor's birthday, Tom's birthday, and now the sorrowful end of two loved one's lives just a year apart—Danie's and Tom's. What an oxymoron. I could not explain it if I had all the words in the dictionary.

Like I said earlier, Tom had only been given days or a couple of weeks to live. The nurses were very caring and offered as much comfort as they could during this difficult time. The Palatable Care Nurse even brought me a red prayer shawl usually made for hospice patients. My pastor, close friends, and my prayer partners showed up to lend their support. My son, son-in-law, and granddaughter brought comfort during this somber time in our lives as well.

I was heartbroken, but I had to keep part of my composure. Jayla was in the waiting room, and I did not want to upset her too much. A doctor came in and pronounced Tom's time of death, but I did not leave the room because Jamus and Pastor Massey wanted to come in and bid Tom farewell.

I felt like I was in a recurring nightmare, similar to the movie, *Groundhog Day*. I was numb and had little feeling about anything. My mind was so confused that at this writing I cannot remember what I did the hours immediately following Tom's death. Jamus and Jayla left and went back to Albany so they could prepare to return for the funeral in a few days. We had not yet determined when that would be, it was too soon. I went home to make calls to my family and Tom's. There was so much sadness and disbelief; people, particularly in the church, had a hard time believing that he passed.

I had to dig deep and trust in a power that I knew I did not possess on my own. I called on the God of my Salvation—Jesus is His name. I had enough confidence to know that if Jesus could not fix the hole in my heart, then nobody could!

Don't forget to say your prayers . . .

Before the storms of life come, *during* the midst of the storm, and *when* you have come through the storm.

God's Assurance to the Broken Hearted

Remember, your Heavenly Father promised to dry up all your tears.

Psalm 147:3 (KJV) *"He heals the brokenhearted and binds up their wounds."*

Psalm 56:8 (MSG) *"You've kept track of my every toss and turn through sleepless nights. Each tear entered in your ledger, each ache written in your book."*

(Isaiah 61:1 (AMP) *"The Lord . . . has sent me to bind up and heal the brokenhearted."*

Revelation 21: 3–5 (MSG) reminds us of the eternal joy and comfort that shall be bestowed upon all believers. *"I heard a voice thunder from the Throne: 'Look! Look! God has moved into the neighborhood, making his home with men and women! They're his people, he's their God. He'll wipe every tear from their eyes. Death is gone for good—tears gone, crying gone. Pain gone—all the first order of things gone." The enthroned continued, 'Look! I'm making everything new. Write it all down—each word dependable and accurate.'"*

STORM CHASING REFLECTIONS

(This page is provided for you to reflect on how you can apply what you've read to help you get through the storm.)

CHAPTER TWO

CAREST THOU NOT IF I PERISH?

The days and months following my daughter's death were—to say the least—difficult, lonely, sad, and unbearable at times. The outpouring of love and support was overwhelming at times. I felt like I was in this prayer cocoon and masses of people were praying for my family's survival. We were mostly concerned with how Jamus was going to fare following the tremendous loss of his wife and mother of his infant daughter. The troops rallied around him and promised to be there to do what they could to provide the practical help that one needs to rebuild one's life. Jayla needed a caregiver during the day; she needed someone to take care of her hair. And Jamus needed soul support and counseling to help him get over the initial shock of losing his soul mate. Tom and I had to grapple with losing our first child, the one whom God ordained to live even though the doctor proclaimed her life would end in miscarriage like my two previous pregnancies.

My mom had to face the stark reality that she had just buried another loved one that was so near and dear to her. She buried a young son, a husband, and now a grandchild. I worried that this death would be the one that would take my mother over the edge. However, to my surprise, her strength is what helped to carry me throughout the whole process. In fact, she took the initial blow when Danielle passed because she was at her bedside.

I was no stranger to storms. In my first book, I talked about some of them. Even from my youth the storms of life began to blow across the canvas of my life; the difference is that these storms were spaced, and they came during different seasons in my life. There were periods of refreshing. Jobs, ministry, school, relationships, were made available to distract and motivate me to continue the path the Lord had me on. I was engaged in things that took my mind off of my pain. Later in my adult life, I began to seek a more intimate relationship with God, so my motives and aspirations became less Lydia-centered and became more God-centered.

Despite my growing relationship with the Lord, much of the time I spent in church as an adult was still worked related, with less and less time focused on building a relationship. Sometimes we in the church will use ministry to hide or mask our pain. We seldom seek the deliverance needed to be set free from the weight and the sin that so easily ensnares us. We believe that most healings occur supernaturally, through prayer, fasting, faith, and church attendance. However, I beg to differ with you! Some of us need to seek counseling, get some doctor-ordered prescription medication, call on God for deliverance while at the altar, and go somewhere and sit down. We need God to speak a word of wisdom for our circumstances.

Again as I said before, I was used to storms coming in and out of my life. By the grace of God, I was able to chronicle and channel some of my pain in the numerous journals that I kept, so you see writing was not a new thing to me. It definitely brought about some healing, but there was more that needed to be done. The hurt you experience from losing a daughter and then a husband was no surface cut that was easily healed. There were deep scars! My insides were ripped apart.

I went back to work five or six weeks after Danielle's death. Trying to work, minister, and be a wife was not an easy task. I continued to pray, attend church, and continue some of my ministry duties, but it was extremely hard. Friends offered to come over to talk, take me to dinner, go shopping or do whatever I wanted to do. They did not want me to be alone and suffer in silence. I did not seek counseling, and that was a big mistake. My husband and I could not fix each other. In some cases, we became distant from each other. We did not want to get in each other's way. We were both hurt and messed up on the inside, and neither one of us wanted to admit that to the other. There were times when he caught me crying and comforted me the best he could. Tom was unemployed, so he spent many days at home alone following Danie's death. He never showed too much emotion while he was around me. However, I know there was an ache inside of him that never healed.

He saw his baby girl in so much pain for 14 months. He told me of a time in the hospital that she reached out for him and said, "Daddy, help me." Those words were indelibly etched in his mind. He told me that it tore him apart, because there was nothing he could do to take away her pain. I think my husband died of a broken heart. The desire to help his baby girl was so great that it just consumed him. Tom never took his pain out on other people. Though he was an emotional and sensitive guy, he didn't let others into his personal hell. He didn't confide in too many people. He and I were best friends, and we shared secrets and were pretty honest about what was going on in our lives, individually and collectively. Most of the time, Tom was content. He said that God had blessed him to realize his dreams. He was in love with his wife, and he had two children and a granddaughter whom he absolutely adored. What could be better than that? He was joyful, loved the church and God's people. When he smiled, that big wide face lit up the whole room. When he laughed, it was like the roar of thunder rolling across the sky. He made everybody feel better by just being in his midst.

No one could have told me that I would have to make another journey to hell and back within a years' time of the passing of my daughter. I didn't believe it was possible for my name to come up again, in terms of God allowing another faith test. I heard R. A. Vernon, Pastor of the Word Church in Cleveland, Ohio preach about Job some time ago. He was preaching a sermon series called *The Survivor's Series* and one night he was ministering on the test that God's servant Job went through. The message was entitled *My Name Came Up.* In the message, Pastor Vernon talked about how Satan and God had a conversation about Job. The Lord actually made a recommendation to Satan regarding Job.

> *8 "Then the Lord said to Satan, "Have you considered my servant Job, that there is none like him on the earth, a blameless and upright man, one who fears God and shuns evil?" 9 So Satan answered the Lord and said, "Does Job fear God for nothing?" 10 "Have you not made a hedge around him around his household, and around all that he has on every side? You have blessed the work of his hands, and his possessions have increased in the land. 11 "But now stretch out your hand and touch all that he has*

and he will surely curse You to Your face!" (Job1:8–11 NKJV)

What the devil was saying was that Job feared the Lord and worshipped Him because of the blessings God had given him, but the minute these blessings are taken away Job would curse Jehovah to His face. I identified with the sermon because Job's name did not come up because he sinned. In fact, Scripture points out that Job was an upright man, who feared God and kept away from evil. What struck me was God pointing out Job's integrity to the devil and subsequently, allowing the devil to destroy Job's family and take away all of his material possessions.

Sometimes God allows Satan to test our faith in God. Sometimes God wants to see if His recommendation of us will stand the test of family, finance, position, power and influence, relationships, personal ministry, etc. To tell you the truth, some of us come more highly recommended than others! The minute we say to God, "Lord, I want to be used of You mightily. Lord, I want more of your spirit. Lord whatever you ask me to do, my answer will be yes!" The minute we say yes to the Lord, we set ourselves up for trouble to knock at our door. I said in *Don't Forget to Say Your Prayers*, that I never knew my *yes* would cost so much. However, we have to realize that knowing God means we must know Him in the power of His resurrection, in His fellowship, and in His suffering.

I wasn't aware that my name came up the first time, but I had, by the grace of God, begun to accept that God was and is "Sovereign." He can do whatever He wants to do when He wants to, and how He wants to. God doesn't owe me any explanation, and He doesn't have to ask my permission! The thing that floored me was like Job, my name came up a second time! After the Lord allowed the devil to destroy Job's family, take away all of his wealth and possessions, Job still held onto his integrity. In verse 21 he says: "Naked I came from my mother's womb, and naked shall I return there. The Lord gave, and the Lord has taken away; "Blessed be the name of the LORD." (Job 1:21 NKJV)

In the second chapter of Job, Satan presents himself *again* before the Lord and the Lord asked him (paraphrased), "What's up, what are you doing and where are you going?" Satan responds, "From going to and fro on the earth, and from walking back and forth on it." (Job 2:2 NKJV) I imagine God must have had His chest poked out when He said to Satan:

> [3] *"Have you considered My servant Job, that there is none like him on the earth, a blameless and upright man, one who fears God and shuns evil? And still he holds fast to his integrity, although you incited Me against him, to destroy him without cause."* [4] *So Satan answered the Lord and said, "Skin for skin! Yes, all that a man has he will give*

for his life. [5]But stretch out Your hand now, and touch his bone and his flesh, and he will surely curse You to Your face!" (Job 2: 3–5 NKJV)

I have read that part of Job before, but this story did not come alive until I heard Pastor Vernon expound on it. Now it makes sense to me just a little more. It astounded me when the Lord brought up Job's name again. Hadn't Job suffered through enough? Why did God insist upon bragging about him further to the devil? God, with His infinite knowledge, knew that Job could be trusted with this trial. He knows the beginning from the ending. Job did not disappoint God. He went through whatever he had to go through—all while listening to his jacked-up friends tell him he must have done something that ticked God off. They came, one by one, to reason with Job in hopes he would break down and confess some sin he had committed. They were certain it was sin that brought this reproach and disaster upon Job's household.

But Job's confession was that during his lifetime he would wait on the Lord. There was a brief moment when Job lost his mind. He started to argue and get angry at God because he could not rationally understand why he was being put through all of these changes. He knew that he had not purposely sin. And, in fact, he was careful to make sacrifices for not only his sins, but for his family's sins as well.

Job and I shared the same frustration. God finally spoke to Job to remind him that He (God) was sovereign. He is the one that keeps the universe in place. He set the stars in the sky, and He controls the temperature. He makes one animal a beast and the other tame. I had my own Job experience. I questioned God. I reminded Him of my devotion to Him. I reminded Him of the prayers that went up to Him faithfully. I reminded Him about His promise to heal the afflicted. I reminded Him daily about the healing Scriptures that, if prayed in faith, would heal the sick. But no matter how much I reminded God of His promises He had the last word.

My name came up because He knew there were some places in my spirit that needed to be connected. There was more pruning that had to take place before the releasing of His power would work in my life to affect many others. He knew there were some false constructs I believed about the Word of God, faith, prayer, and the will of God that had to be straightened out. I would have to go through another storm, but the storm did not come to destroy me; the storm did not come to stay. The storm came so that I would maintain my integrity and conviction that God would be God no matter what. In fact, I should be honored God would even mention my name among the heavenly hosts and before Satan. Like I said earlier, some of us come more highly recommended than others.

I know how the disciples must have felt when they were in the angry seas with the winds and the waves misbehaving. Jesus was with them in the back of the boat, but fear gripped their hearts, and they forgot that the one who calms the seas, walks upon the water, sends rain to desert places, heals all manner of diseases, and raises the dead was in the boat with them. The men cried out, "Careth thou not that we perish?" (Mark 4:38b KJV) Their cries for help awakened Him, and He rebuked them for their lack of faith. How could anything happen to them when Jesus, *God Himself* was in the boat with them?

Jesus is the anchor of our souls. He will allow the storms to come into our lives, but He never leaves us without a life jacket. He is our lifeline. We have His word that He will never leave us or forsake us. When we are in distress, He gets in our boat with us. He rides upon the waves of our circumstances and says: "Peace, be still!" (Mark 4:39a KVJ) I now know when my name came up a second time, God was up to something.

As I said before, my husband's sudden illness took us by surprise. Tom was admitted into the hospital on October 3, 2011. After a myriad of tests, x-rays and evaluations by several different doctors, he was diagnosed with stage 4 lung cancer. There were tumors in both lungs. His illness was complicated by his diabetes and his weight. There was no prescription or treatment that would cure him. We needed a miracle, but would God graciously grant one this time?

As you know by now, the answer to that question was, No! During October there are several important days that we celebrate:

- October 5th is our anniversary.
- October 17th is Trevor's birthday.
- October 21st is Tom's birthday.

We did the best we could to celebrate these days in the hospital with Tom, knowing full well that this was the last time we would celebrate them together. On our anniversary, I bought him a balloon that played the song "You're Still the One." I tapped on the balloon, so he would hear it playing as I was coming down the hallway. When I got into the room, he was smiling from ear to ear! He thought that was so unlike me to do something like that, and it really made his day. However, the anniversary date that does not give us any comfort is October 28th because that is the day that both Danielle and Tom made their transition from earth to heaven.

On October 16, 2012, I began writing my second book. I made the decision to do something creative and purposeful to fulfill my passion for writing. I wanted the first anniversary of Danielle and Tom's deaths to be filled with memories of the great times we spent as a family. I wanted to remember the times Tom and I shared before and after we had our children. I wanted to remember the joy and completeness that Danielle brought to our lives.

I know within my heart that even though the storms keep raging in my life, my anchor is in Jesus! He will bring me across the stormy seas to a land of unlimited love. I am glad that the Book of Job did not end with 41 chapters. In chapter 42, the Bible recounts that God gave Job double for his trouble. Job's days were extended. He had more children and more possessions than he had before. God is a God of restoration. He promises that if we are willing to give up everything for the sake of the Gospel, we will not be disappointed. There is a harvest that we will reap if we are faithful. Ephesians 3:20 reminds us that God can do exceedingly, abundantly, more than we can ask, think, or imagine, according to the power that is already working in us.

Sometimes we get it twisted and believe that we are the only ones whom the devil is picking on. We have to remember that the Lord God allows the enemy of our soul, Satan, to have his way with us. In fact, when we are in Christ, he has to ask God's permission to bring affliction upon us.

I don't merely want to survive life's tragedies; I want to be an overcomer—a victor in my circumstances. There are several Scriptures that address the fact that it is possible to recover from the vicissitudes and disastrous situations of life. Someone once said, "When life gives you a lemon, just make lemonade." That is a great way to face life's trials and disappointments. Though it is not healthy to be pessimistic, it is wise to realize you cannot change some things. When the best-ordered plans don't always work out, when you have done your best and have put your faith to work, you have to rest in God's strength just like David did. God will overshadow you with His love, His mercy, and His encouragement.

STORM CHASER

Begin your recovery by praying and reading the following Scriptures.

1Samuel 30:6 (NASB) *"David was greatly distressed . . . But David strengthened himself in the LORD his God."*

Psalm 23:1–3 (KJV) "*The Lord is my shepherd; I shall not want. He makes me lie down in green pastures; He leads me beside the still waters, He restores my soul. He leads me in the paths of righteousness For His name's sake."*

Psalm 27:4–5 (KJV) "*One thing I have desired of the Lord, That will I seek: That I may dwell in the house of the Lord all the days of my life to behold the beauty of the Lord, and inquire in His temple. For in the time of trouble He shall hide me in His pavilion; He shall hide me; He shall set me high upon a rock."*

Psalm 30:5 (NKJV) *"Weeping may endure for a night, but joy comes in the morning.*

Psalm 34:18 (NKJV) *"The Lord is near to those who have a broken heart, And saves such as have a contrite spirit.*

Psalm 46:-1-2 (NKJV) *"God is our refuge and strength, A very present help in trouble. Therefore we will not fear, Even though the earth be removed, And though the mountains be carried into the midst of the sea;*

2 Corinthians 1:3–4 (NKJV) "*Blessed be the God and Father of our Lord Jesus Christ, the Father of mercies and God of all comfort, who comforts us in all our tribulations that we may be able to comfort those who are in any trouble, with the same comfort with which we ourselves are comforted by God.*

Matthew 11:28–30 (NKJV) *"Come to Me, all you who labor and are heavy laden, and I will give you rest. Take My yoke upon you and learn from Me, for I am gentle and lowly in heart, and you will find rest for your souls. For My yoke is easy and my burden is light."*

And as always I remind you: "Don't forget to say your prayers."

STORM CHASING REFLECTIONS

(This page is provided for you to reflect on how you can apply what you've read to help you get through the storm.)

CHAPTER THREE

DEVIL, GOD BLOCKED IT!

In the midst of all the sad news concerning my husband's terminal illness, there loomed a serious situation I faced concerning the living conditions of my home. Our home was built in the late fifties. We purchased it in 1994, and many of the structures were the original structures, i.e.: windows, doors, kitchen cabinetry, built-in oven, range top, furnace, etc. The only visible upgrades to the house were the siding, a finished basement, freshly painted walls, and a carpet that looked fairly new. When we moved in the roof was in good condition, but over the span of fifteen years it had begun to deteriorate and needed to be repaired. Water damage seeped in through the foundation in the basement. Our sump pump worked, but occasionally storms caused it to overflow and water seeped into the lower level of the house.

Over time we noticed a recurrent dampness and smell of mold in our basement. The rug in our lower bedroom would be damp whenever it stormed badly or there was extended rainfall. The closet smelled of mildew, and my clothes had a moldy smell to them. Tom and I had begun to investigate ways of addressing the water damage that was occurring throughout the house. Several times we engaged a plumber to fix problems we were having with tubs, sinks and water seeping through the ceiling into the family room. Some water damage caused cracks and damage to the ceiling in the family room.

Tom and I researched the effects of having mold build up in your home. I began to wonder if his illness was connected to the results of having mold infestation in the lower part of our house. In fact, I was in the process of having a mold inspection while Tom was hospitalized.

I was aware there was a storm headed towards Connecticut. The meteorologist had predicted the storm would arrive around October 29th, come in, drop a few inches of precipitation, with some high winds and then be out as quickly as it came in. I was afraid more rain would cause further water damage in our basement. Throughout his short illness, Tom had encouraged me to continue to follow through with the mold inspection and resolve the situation in our home.

In preparation for the storm, I went out and purchased some supplies. The next day I cleaned out my refrigerator because I suspected that people would begin coming to pay their respects and bring food as is the custom in the Black Church. In our culture, we always celebrate deaths and funerals around food.

My spiritual daughter called me and offered to do some shopping for me, but I told her that wasn't necessary. Then my best friend, Angela showed up and insisted on going shopping for me. When she returned we put the food away. It had already begun snowing. A few church members showed up and dropped off chicken and other types of food. My refrigerator was filling up. However, once the morning hours passed, the weather report shifted. Meteorologists started saying the storm was going to be worse than had been predicted earlier. It was fall, and the leaves were still on the trees. I can see them outside of my window as I write these words. Now meteorologists were predicting not only snow but extremely high winds as well. They were afraid that the winds would cause many of the leaves, branches, and trees to fall, thus causing damage to power lines across the state. The storm had been named, "Storm Alfred."

Alfred was turning into be a major nor'easter. Who would have guessed that we would have this type of weather in October? It was October 29th and children all over the state were preparing for Halloween in just a couple of days. By late afternoon, the snow was starting to stick to the ground. The winds had picked up, and leaves were becoming packed with snow. The heaviness of the leaves on the trees caused many branches in my yard and around the state to snap, crackle, and pop. Huge trees were uprooted and toppled into yards and streets all over the state.

The meteorologists were constantly updating and changing their earlier forecast. Earlier, I called my friend Wanda, who lived in Albany, New York, because she was preparing to drive to my home. I warned her about the weather and told her to be extremely careful in her journey to get to me. She was determined that she was going to be here to comfort and care for me. Meanwhile, Angela and I sat around talking about Tom, Danielle and the events that had transpired during the last 14 months. I made sure I had candles, flashlights, and a charged cell phone along with my land line phone. We certainly were not going to starve because the refrigerator was packed with food.

As night drew nearer, we could hear the effects the wind and the heavy weight the leaves had on the trees. We tried to take a nap, but I awaken to the popping sound of the branches just outside my window. In fact, there was a smaller tree in front of my picture window that snapped in two and lay not far from my window. Angela and I stayed abreast of the weather forecasts regarding Storm Alfred. We were starting to get a little concerned. The electricity went out around eight or nine o'clock. I went out a couple of times to charge my phone in my car. The land line phone worked most of the evening, but then we lost complete power.

Earlier, I brought up a cooler and filled it with meat and perishable foods. I put it out on the deck to keep it cold. Finally, we went to bed. I went to my bedroom, and Angie stayed downstairs on the couch. The next morning, we were still tired, cold and stunned by the damage the storm had caused. I reached my son, and he told me that he had electricity in East Hartford. So, we made plans to pack up some food and head over there. The night before, I was in touch with Wanda, who I finally convinced to get off the highway. I told her that once she got into Springfield, Massachusetts she needed to check into a hotel and stay there until morning. Luckily, she found one that was opened and had limited electrical power. Well, morning finally came, hallelujah! Wanda called to let me know she was alright, and I proceeded to give her instructions on how to get to my house. We met at a gas station in Bloomfield and headed over to Trevor's house in East Hartford.

We turned his small apartment into a hotel for the next few days. My Mom, sister, son-in-law, and granddaughter would also become tenants in Trevor's home in the next few days. The forecast was dim to say the least. There were thousands upon thousands of homes without electricity. The power company had no clue that this storm would paralyze the East Coast to this magnitude. They did not know when complete power would be restored to the region. There were trees and telephone lines down all over the highways, roads, and backyards across the state of Connecticut, and surrounding states. And in the midst of this hellish experience, I would have to make preparations for a funeral.

Tom's body had to remain at the hospital because the funeral home had no electricity. Communication with the funeral home director was limited and sparse. Yes, most people had cell phones, but they needed to be connected to some type of power source. Most people had to resort to charging their phones from their cars. Once Tom passed, we called the funeral hall to engage their services; however, the hospital would have to inform them when the body would be ready to be dismissed and transported from their facility.

Elder Greg Green and his family also lived in East Hartford. Unfortunately, they did not have electricity in the area where they lived. His wife Cookie did the program for my daughter's home going service. I thought it would be a good idea if we started the process, since Trevor's computer was working.

There we were: my son-in-law Jamus, granddaughter Jayla, my friends Angela, Wanda, The Greens, Trevor and his fiancée Allyson. We had a filling meal, discussed the storm, travel plans and a host of other things. After dinner

Cookie and I began to make a rough draft of the program on my son's computer. Later that night, my pastor contacted me and was able to weather the road conditions and made it to Trevor's apartment. His electrical services were out as well. The preliminary details were worked out. All we could do now was wait to be in further contact with the funeral home. We could not schedule the date of the funeral until we knew when services would be restored to the building.

On Monday October 31st, I was able to contact Joann Wiggins, the funeral director. She told me they still did not have any electricity at their facility. I would have to meet them elsewhere to discuss the details of the funeral. My mom had flown in on Monday, and my sister was due to come in on Tuesday. Tuesday morning I returned to my cold dark house, went upstairs to look in our closet and chose suits I thought Tom would look good in. One of his suits was actually in the cleaners, so I stopped there to pay for it and picked it up on my way to meet with Joann. Driving conditions were treacherous throughout Connecticut and especially treacherous in our area. In fact, most of the traffic lights in Bloomfield were out. At various intersections there were some stop signs placed there by the police, but at other corners there were none. People, myself included, had to wait and rely on the kindness of their fellow drivers. It was imperative that drivers acted responsibly and yielded the right of way to others at critical intersections. That way, traffic could proceed with fewer incidents or accidents.

Sometime around 11 or 12 o'clock I got to Windsor Avenue where I finally met with Joann. My son Trevor was present also. On the way to the meeting one of my windshield wipers popped off, and I would have to return to Bloomfield to get a new one. I knew of a beauty shop located on Windsor Avenue and decided to stop to see if the owner was busy. She didn't have any customers, so I asked her if she could do my hair after my meeting, and she said, "Yes."

It was around four o'clock when I left the beauty shop. As I was leaving, I learned that it was going to cost five hundred dollars to place the obituary in the Hartford Courant. I was shocked at the cost! I could not understand why it cost so much. I was still fussing about that when I left the shop. I got in my car and proceeded down Windsor Avenue with the intent to make a U-turn and go back to Bloomfield to get a new windshield wiper. Thank God the lights were working in this part of town. When I approached the intersection of Windsor Ave and Barber Street, I saw a green light, and I was about to make a left turn. To my horror, I forgot to allow the traffic the right of way, and I turned in front of a car. I was terrified! I began screaming because I saw the driver coming towards me. I just knew I was going to die. The oncoming car slammed into the side of my car and both of the airbags came out! I accelerated in hopes of getting out of the way so that I would not take a direct hit. I managed to turn my car into a grove of trees and applied the brake so that I didn't run into the trees. There was a police car right in back of the driver, and the officer saw everything. Clearly, it was my fault; I caused the accident!

Once my car came to a complete stop, I looked down at my right hand which was swollen ten times its size. I was in excruciating pain. The police officer that witnessed the accident came over and told me he had to give me a ticket *because* he had witnessed everything. The ambulance was called because the driver in the car that hit me was injured. He had to be taken to the hospital by ambulance. I called my son and a couple of friends who came to the scene of the accident. Trevor took me to the hospital, and my friends came along as well. Thank God the examination showed that there were no broken bones in my hand. I had some contusions and muscle spasms, but I would live. All that week Jessie, Carrie, and Ruby insisted if I needed to drive anywhere or make arrangements, they would be glad to help me out. I insisted I was alright, and I did not need their assistance. The accident certainly proved otherwise.

My hand was bandaged up, but my life was spared. I immediately thought the devil put a hit on me and wanted to wipe me off the face of the earth. His plan was to make my son fatherless and motherless in one fell swoop. But the devil is a liar! GOD blocked it! He would not let it be so. If the enemy had a plan to take me out, God had another plan. And His plan said, "You will live and not die." I know now that no matter what the devil tries to do to destroy our lives, there's a God that is much greater. He will deliver our feet from falling. Yes, I made a terrible mistake in my judgment. I should not have been driving in the first place. My mind was not focused. I was still in a fog and numbed by the events of my husband's death. Yet, God spared my life! The car was beyond repair, but I came out of that damaged vehicle with only a bruised hand.

However, I don't want to minimize the extent to which my hand was injured. It was my right hand. I had just finished writing my first book. I thought to myself, "Satan is after my gift as well. He would be happy if there was some permanent damage to my hand so that I could not continue to write more books." But the devil is a liar. God blocked that too. After six months of therapy on my hand, I continue to write! I just want to give praise to such an awesome, mighty, powerful God. Nothing can stop the destiny that God has for my life. These books are not just books written to tell a cute emotional story. These books are going to be someone's saving grace. These books are going to literally bring someone back from the brink of losing their mind, committing suicide, leaving their faith, and giving up on life. These life-changing events can leave us desperate, lonely, hopeless and lifeless. The experience of losing a loved one to cancer, murder, divorce or some other type of loss can take months and years to process and recover from.

This was a storm of tumultuous devastation. My husband's life was taken away and translated to its new home in heaven. My life following his death took a further toll on me in that I had to take responsibility for cleaning up the physical damage left from the storm. In addition to that, I had to nurse a bruised right hand which limited the amount of work I could do around the house. Preparations for the funeral were extremely stressful under these conditions, not to mention trying to find housing for my out-of-town family members.

In my mind, I had to grapple with the emotional upheaval of going forward with our son's wedding in a few weeks—a joyous event Tom and I were much anticipating. Additionally, we had to find words of comfort to say to a little two-year girl who had lost her mommy the year before, and now her beloved Papa was gone. There had to be a divinely inspired word that would find a place in her spirit to receive the message that her mom and her Papa were enjoying one another in the heavenly kingdom with Jesus. But who would be able to share that with her?

The Ford and Fulton family on Silver Lane would continue to exist temporarily in the tight living quarters of my son's apartment until we could return to my home in

Bloomfield. Until then, the dreaded tasks of making funeral arrangements, contacting the car rental company to obtain a vehicle, and enduring the emotional stress of making telephone calls to people and other agencies was before me. But God was in the midst of everything. God left His footprints in the sand. The weight of this storm would not deter His promises and plan for my life. God was about to reach down, scoop me up in His arms, and carry me through Storm Alfred and my own personal storm: the story of the back to back tragic endings of the two most significant people in my life, Tom and Danielle.

STORM CHASER

Don't forget to say your prayers before the storms of life come, during the midst of the storm, and when you have come through the storm.

Sometimes when we go through the trials and sufferings of life we think that God has abandoned us. We perceive that maybe He has gone away on vacation, or that He is asleep as far as our circumstances are concerned. Others feel guilty and think that they are being punished for some unrepentant sin they committed and now God is extremely angry with them. But these perceptions about God are false. It is easy to point our finger at God or shake our fist at Him in frustration when something out of the ordinary happens to our loved ones. The natural question is to ask: "Where are you God?" Where are you in all of this mess? Where are you in my daughter's cancer? Where are you in my husband's cancer? Where are you in this car accident? Where are you in my joblessness? Where are you in my son's disability?

God has promised us an abundant lifestyle, yet He has allowed us to be thrown into the chilly river of Jordan seemingly without a life jacket. But, be of good cheer. The Bible tells us that God is in the tough stuff! He can and He will deliver His people. Be encouraged as you read these Scriptures on how God takes care of those who have experienced loss, pain, and suffering. I want you to know my brother and my sister that God is listening, indeed He cares, and is concerned about you!

Read the following Scriptures to help you hold on to the victory that is yours in Christ Jesus.

Psalm 34:17 (ESV) *"When the righteous cry for help, the Lord hears and delivers them out of all their troubles.*

Psalm 107:6 (ESV) *"Then they cried to the Lord in their trouble, and he delivered them from their distress.*

2 Samuel 22:2 (ESV) *"He said, 'The Lord is my rock and my fortress and my deliver.'"*

Jeremiah 1:7–8 (ESV) *"But the Lord said to me, 'Do not say, I am only a youth; for to all to whom I sent you, you shall go, and whatever I command you, you shall speak. Do not be afraid of them, for I am with you to deliver you, declares the Lord.'"*

2 Peter 2:9 (ESV) *"Then the Lord knows how to rescue the godly from trials, and to keep the unrighteous under punishment until the Day of Judgment."*

2 Samuel 22:1 (ESV) *"And David spoke to the Lord the words of this song on the day when the Lord delivered him from the hand of all his enemies and from the hand of Saul."*

1 Peter5:10 (ESV) " . . . *and after you have suffered a little while, the God of all grace, who has called you to his eternal glory in Christ, will himself restore, confirm, strengthen, and establish you."*

Psalm 34:17–20 (ESV) *"When the righteous cry for help, the Lord hears and delivers them out of all their troubles. The Lord is near to the broken hearted and saves the crushed in spirit. Many are the afflictions of the righteous, but the Lord delivers him out of them all. He keeps all his bones; not one of them is broken.*

2 Corinthians 12:9 (ESV) *"But he said to me, "My grace is sufficient for you, for my power is made perfect in weakness, so that the power of Christ may rest upon me."*

Never forget that God knows firsthand what it is like to suffer. His will is not always the easiest, but it is always the best. Sometimes God chooses the most unlikely ways to accomplish His purpose in your life. Any good or bad that we experience here on earth will pale in comparison to what awaits us in eternity.

And as always I remind you: "Don't forget to say your prayers."

STORM CHASING REFLECTIONS

(This space is provided for you to reflect on how you can apply what you've read)

CHAPTER FOUR

FAITH THAT IS NOT TESTED IS NOT FAITH

Abraham is called the "Father of Faith." In chapter 4 of the Book of Romans, Paul explains that Abraham pleased God through faith alone before he ever heard about the rituals and laws that would become so important to the Jewish people. We too are saved by faith plus nothing! It is not by loving God and doing good deeds that we are saved; neither is it by faith plus love nor by faith plus good deeds. We are saved only through faith in Christ, trusting him to forgive our sins.

Abraham never doubted that God would fulfill His promise that Abraham would be the father of many nations (Genesis 17: 2–4) and the entire world would he blessed through him (Genesis 12:3). This promise was fulfilled in Jesus Christ. Jesus was from Abraham's line, and truly the whole world would be blessed through him.

Abraham never doubted God would fulfill His promise to him. His life was marked by mistakes, sin, failures, wisdom, and goodness; however, Abraham was consistent in trusting God. His faith was strengthened by the obstacles he faced, and his life was an example of faith in action. If he had looked only at his own resources and his own body for securing the promises of God, he would have been discouraged and would have given up hope. But Abraham looked to God, obeyed God, and waited for God to fulfill His promise.

What we have to learn as Christians is our faith will be put on trial! Faith that is not put to the test is not faith. Christians have been sold a bill of goods by some church leaders. These false teachers have preached the prosperity message so much and have given people the notion that Christians are not supposed to go through anything. All we need to do is sow our seed/money and look for showers of blessings to fall from the sky. Too much prosperity teaching has made us lazy, complacent, and looking for the pie in the sky blessing. Not only that, but it weakens in our faith and stunts our growth as a Christian.

What we need is a balanced gospel. We need to tell people that God is in the blessing business, but the way He tests our character is by the way of the cross. God is not going to open His hands and pour out a blessing on those who do not have the integrity and character to build up His kingdom. God tells us in His Word that we will be persecuted for His name sake. So then, how do we know that our faith amounts to anything in God's sight? Well, I am glad you asked! Abraham is a perfect example of a man that pleased God—which should be our goal—to please God. Hebrews 11:6 tells us how much God values our faith. It says: "But without faith it is impossible to please Him, for he who comes to God must believe that He is, and that He is a rewarder of those who diligently seek Him."

In the Book of Genesis, Abraham is rewarded for his faith. He and his wife Sarah are given the son whom the Lord promised them. Both were well beyond the age of childbearing. Abraham was 100 and Sarah was 90 or 91 years old. (Genesis 21:1–8) Nevertheless, God brought forth a mighty miracle on Abraham's behalf and Sarah conceived a child. Sarah's take on this whole miracle was expressed this way: "God has made me laugh, and all who hear will laugh with me." She also said, "Who would have said to Abraham that Sarah would nurse children? For I have borne him a son in his old age." (Genesis 21:6–8) NKJV.

However, in the very next chapter the Bibles says: "Now it came to pass after these things that God tested Abraham, and said to him, "Abraham!" and he said, "Here I am." Then He said, "Take now you son, your only son Isaac, whom you love, and go to the land of Moriah, and offer him there as a burnt offering, on one of the mountains of which I shall tell you." (Genesis 22:1–2)

Now this is where the rubber meets the road! Abraham has waited until he was almost 110 years old for this promise of God to come to fruition, and now God asks him to kill Isaac and offer him up as a sacrifice to God. Most of us would be like, "Ah, God talk to the hand because the ear is not listening." No parent in their right mind would be willing to lay hands on their own child and take his or her life. But that is exactly what God was asking Abraham to do. Again, a faith that is not tested is not faith. James says it like this, "Faith without works is dead."(James 2:26). A dead faith is worse than no faith at all. Faith must work; it must produce; it must be visible. Verbal faith is not enough; mental faith is insufficient. Faith must be there, but it must be more. It must inspire action. James emphasizes throughout this chapter that true faith must manifest itself in some corresponding action.

The Bible tells us that Abraham proceeded to follow through with God's command. When he got to the designated place, he told the young men who traveled with him, "Stay here with the donkey; the lad and I will go yonder and worship, and we will come back to you." (Genesis 22: 5–6)

I love Abraham's response right here because it shows his confidence and trust in God. He doesn't tell the young men that he is going to make a sacrifice; he tells them that he is going to worship. This lets me know that whenever you are getting ready for a test or to do a hard thing, you need to worship. Worship brings God's presence and power into the circumstance. Worship is the warfare that is needed to take the heat out of the fire. Worship is a song, your devotion, that which touches and melts the heart of God. Worship is what brings about the delivering mercy and compassion of God in your direction.

When Abraham makes ready the altar, Isaac responds that he sees the fire and the wood, but questions his father as to where the sacrifice/animal is. Again, I love Abraham's answer to his son: "My son God will provide for Himself the lamb for the burnt offering," so the two of them went together (Genesis 22:8). Abraham was, in my opinion, the man of the hour. He got it right. He believed that God was going to keep His word. He promised him that a whole nation would come from his loins. Abraham believed God was not a man that could or would lie.

Then they came to the place where the sacrifice was to be made. He tied Isaac and placed him on the altar. He lifted up the knife to slay his son. But the Angel of the Lord called to him from heaven and said, "Abraham, Abraham!" So he said, "Here I am." And He said, "Do not lay your hand on the lad or do anything to him: for now I know that you fear God, since you have not withheld your son, your only son, from Me." Then Abraham lifted his eyes and looked, and there behind him was a ram caught in a thicket by its horns. So Abraham went and took the ram, and offered it up for a burnt offering instead of his son. (Genesis 22:10–13)

If you read the remainder of chapter 22, you will find that God was very pleased with Abraham. He reiterates the blessings that He has in store for him as a result of his love and obedience. He promises that He will multiply Abraham's descendants as the stars of the heaven and as the sand which is on the seashore. He also promises to protect Abraham's descendants from their enemies. God says, "In your seed all the nations of the earth shall be blessed, because you have obeyed My voice. (Genesis 22:18)

At some point, yours and my faith will be tested! God places such a high value on our faith. The Apostle Peter puts it this way:

> *"These trials are only to test your faith, to show that it is strong and pure. It is being tested as fire tests and purifies gold—and your faith is far more precious to God than mere gold. So if your faith remains strong after being tried by fiery trials, it will bring you much praise and glory and honor on the day when Jesus Christ is revealed to the whole world."* (1 Peter 1:7 NLT)

When people go to court, they are put on trial. Their veracity in the truth of a matter will find them either guilty or innocent. The case is presented by two opposing attorneys—namely the prosecutor and the defense attorney, respectively. Each is looking for corroborating evidence to find his or her client guilty or not guilty. A jury is selected to hear the case. They must listen to all the evidence. After it has all been presented, they get together and go over both the prosecutor's and the defense attorney's arguments. At the appropriate time, the jury renders a verdict based on the evidence.

The fact that your faith and my faith are on trial means there exists some evidence that it is either present or absent. God puts our faith to the test so that He can see how well the evidence will hold up in His court of faith. Our faith must be tested. It cannot be wishy-washy. We can't allow our emotions to dictate our belief system. Emotions are like the weather and the weather changes from day to day. Faith that is emotional is not steady. James warns us about unsteady faith in (James 1:7–8) NKJV:

> *"But let him ask in faith, with no doubting, for he who doubts is like a wave of the sea driven and tossed by the wind. For let not that man suppose that he will receive anything from the Lord; he is a double-minded man, unstable in all his ways."*

God is clear on this issue. Without faith, you cannot expect to receive anything from the Lord. There is no need to pray if you do not have faith. When you pray, you should expect to receive those things that you pray for. If you don't believe that God has the power to bring those things to pass, your prayers and your faith are worthless. I don't know about you, but I expect to have my prayers answered by God. I expect to receive the goodness and blessings that God has in store for me in the land of the living. Yes, I know there are treasures laid up in heaven for me, but I want to reap some of God's goodness while my feet are still on this earth.

The truth is those good things are always appropriated by faith. I believe my faith has been tested and I have passed the test. Even though things did not turn out the way I would have liked them, I still believe that God knows what is best for me. I still believe that my best days are ahead of me. I refuse to continue to question God about why He allowed my daughter and husband to die from cancer. I refuse to become bitter and angry because I now have to go through life wondering if I did something wrong to cause their deaths. The devil will not trick me into believing that I caused their demise. I will not be fooled into thinking that I did not have enough faith to believe God for a miracle. I will not curse God or turn my back on Him. "Though He slay me, yet will I trust Him." (Job 13:15 NKJV)

Faith endures trials. Trials come and go, but a strong faith will face them head-on and develop endurance. Faith understands temptations. It will not allow us to consent to our lust and slide into sin. Faith obeys the Word. It will not merely hear and not do. Faith produces a corresponding action. It is demonstrated by obedience, and it overtly responds to the promises of God. It produces the ability to resist the devil and humbly draw near to God. Finally, faith waits patiently for the coming of the Lord; through trouble and trial, it stifles the urge to complain and feel sorry for oneself.

I refuse to be a victim of my circumstances. I am a powerful overcoming, faith believing woman of God. I pray that these words will find fertile soil within your heart. I pray that they will inspire you to continue to contend for the faith. Satan is our enemy and the thing he hates the most is our faith. If he can steal our faith, he has won the battle for our salvation. The Bible says, "The just shall live by faith." (Habbakuk 2:4 NKJV). Those are good words to uphold and build one's life around. Grab a hold on them and refuse to let go. Be empowered my brother and my sister.

STORM CHASER

Don't forget to say your prayers when . . .

You feel like you are sinking into the abyss; when you feel like you are being kept from obtaining the peace, love, truth, and purposes of God; when you feel like you are being held captive by your own emotions as a result of experiencing abandonment, rejection, or any type of loss. Remember these words and decree and declare over your life these words:

Isaiah 26:3 (KVJ) *"Thou will keep him in perfect peace, whose mind is stayed on thee; because he trusteth in thee.*

Paul said these words to his protégé Timothy:
2 Timothy 1:12 (KJV) *"For the which cause I also suffer these things: nevertheless I am not ashamed: for I know whom I have believed, and am persuaded that he is able to keep that which I have committed unto him against that day."*

When the wicked one is harassing your thoughts confess, decree, declare and affirm these words in your spirit:

1 Samuel 2:9 (KJV) *"He will keep the feet of his saints, and the wicked shall be silent in darkness for Every word of God is pure: he is a shield unto them that put their trust in him."*

Psalms 41:2 (KJV) *"The Lord will preserve him and keep him alive, and he will be blessed on the earth; You will not deliver him to the will of his enemies.*

John 15:7 (KJV) "*Blessed are they that hear the Word of God and keep it."*

STORM CHASING REFLECTIONS

(This space is provided for you to reflect on how you can apply what you've read)

CHAPTER FIVE

OH, TO BE KEPT BY JESUS

There is a gospel hit song written by Kurt Carr entitled: "I Almost Let Go." The words describe the emotional roller-coaster that one goes through when they are immersed in great pain and agony. The hurt is so deep, so intense, you feel like giving up and throwing in the towel. Going to church, praying, fasting and fellowshipping with the saints is far from your mind. In fact, if one more person recites another Scripture you may knock the Be-Jesus out of them! This deep dark place that I went to when I lost both my loved ones was a dangerous place. On several occasions the devil had me thinking that I could really just drive my car off the Massachusetts Turnpike down a cliff and end my life. I never told anyone but Syrette that I thought about ending my life at some point. That was not the spiritual words of a preacher that anyone would justify, nope not by any means. But truly, I almost let go, but in my weakened state, the Holy Ghost held onto me, encouraged me, comforted and spoke peace to my soul. Goodness and Mercy carried me when I couldn't see my way. The Lord picked me up and carried me through one of the darkest periods in my life. The Bible says: "He will keep that which is committed to Him against that day, or until Jesus comes back." (2 Timothy 1:12 KJV). I thank God for keeping me and breathing life back into this lifeless body of mine.

Before Kurt Carr was born and before there was a medium called *Contemporary Gospel*, there was an old hymn entitled: "Oh to Be Kept" by Michael Fletcher. The words of that song are:

Oh to be kept, by Jesus, Kept by the power of God.
Kept, from the world unspotted,
treading where Jesus trod.

Oh to be kept by Jesus. Lord at Thy feet I fall.
I would be nothing, nothing, nothing.
Thy shalt be all and all.

It gives me great comfort and assurance to know God is the one who grabs and holds on to you. When you are in the midst of the storm, there are some strange feelings, events and circumstances that can be all consuming. If your soul is not anchored in Jesus, you will lose your footing and slip further into the abyss.

Following the death of my daughter, Danielle in 2010, I struggled to pull myself out of the deep sorrow and devastation that I felt. I was grateful to God for my granddaughter, Jayla, who I believe was God's gift to our entire family. Nothing that happens to us in life comes as a surprise to God. We give the devil too much credit for the terrible trials and tribulations that we endure. However, the truth is everything that happens to us is filtered through the permissive will of God! God is not this enormous ogre in the sky that purposely wreaks havoc on our lives. The Lord does not waste any of our life's experiences. He uses them to perfect our character, increase our faith, and expose us to catastrophic circumstances so that we can use the wisdom we obtained to help others. God takes us through and brings us out of the fire so we will have a testimony. The test is not for ourselves, but there are others who will experience some of the same circumstances that we just came through.

The toughest lesson I had to learn from the deaths of my daughter and husband was God is sovereign! He is not Santa Clause or a genie. He will not be bossed or manipulated! He does not care about your race, religion, culture, title, position, rules, traditions, and commandments. We don't get to decide who should suffer, get sick, healed or die; all decisions are left up to God. They were decided upon before the foundation of the world! It doesn't matter how much Holy Ghost you think you have, or if you can pray like Peter, Silas or Paul, the Bible says: "Time and chance happens to all men." (Ecclesiastes 9:11) If you live long enough, you are going to go through something. Again, the Bible says:" Many are the afflictions of the righteous, but The Lord delivers them from them all." (Psalms 34:19 KJV).

I am not saying that God doesn't require us or expect us to exercise our faith in Him or pray with thanksgiving and expectation in our heart. We should pray and fast individually and corporately. But we should not play God, or place the burden of our prayers not being answered in the way we would have liked them answered on our shoulders. If God healed and worked miracles in the lives of our loved ones based upon our "works," we might get the big head and really think that we are all that, a bag of chips, and hot sauce on the side! Rather, we are His chosen vessels whom He chooses to use according to His purpose. "For it is God which worketh in you both to will and to do of his good pleasure" (Philippians 2:13 KJV).

I spent the last 20 years of my life chasing after God and pursuing my purpose in life. My desire as a worshipper and intercessor was to know Christ and develop a close relationship with Him. Being faithful to my calling, submitting to leadership in the church, and conducting myself in a godly manner were things that I tried to adhere to. As a minister, I attended many funerals, visited the sick and shut-in, ministered at convalescent homes, etc. At funerals, I read the Scripture, prayed the prayer of comfort, and comforted the bereaved families. I did what ministers are trained to do! But when death comes knocking at your door, it is a different story.

I had already lost a brother while in my twenties. My father was seventy-five years old when he passed; I turned fifty the year he died. My grandmother died at the ripe age of ninety-nine. What a blessing! She passed in 2006; I was fifty-five at the time. These deaths were devastating, but at least they were spaced out. Losing Danie and Tom a year apart on the same day was a little too much to bear! No one expects to lose their child—no matter if the child is 3, 30, or 85. I began to think that my experiences were a part of some grand scheme that the devil perpetrated to destroy my life, my ministry, and my destiny.

There were times when I literally thought my soul, the seat of where my emotions lie, would never recover from the loss of Tom and Danielle. Many times I felt empty and worn down. Where was God? I could not feel, find or trace Him. I did not feel the anointing of His glory or power over my life. Sometimes all I could do was lie in a lifeless stupor and curl up in a ball like possums do when they play dead. Was I dead? My heart was still beating, but my soul, mind, body and spirit had abandoned ship. I felt like those who are lost at sea in a damaged ship, beyond repair, and the only hope they have is to get in the lifeboats, float on the water and wait for the Coast Guard to come and rescue them.

But somewhere deep inside my spirit, in that place of the supernatural, there was a power that would not quit. This grace, God's enablement, this awesome ability to look beyond the physical events that was happening in my life took control. This grace responded to the years of prayers, worship, and the Word of God that had been stored up through years of developing an intimate relationship with my Lord Jesus. Though my outward man seemed to be perishing, deep within the new man, God's resurrecting power was being renewed day by day. It was my Spirit-man that was being renewed based upon what I was feeding it. And I was feeding my spirit the Word of God constantly. The Spirit of Truth Himself was at work to will and to do His good pleasure in my life.

It was as if the Spirit of Christ hovered over me during those times when I did not have the strength to pray, worship, work, interact with my family and perform my ministerial duties at church. This life-giving spirit searches the deep, hidden things of God on the inside of us. God's Spirit was keeping me, even when I was not aware that anything significant or spiritual was being kept and awakened on the inside of me.

It was miraculous, to say the least, that I was able to go to school and teach all day. God had strengthened me to continue to go to church and teach my Sunday school class, I also continued to lead my women's support group. By God's grace and power, we were able to organize and have our fifth annual BFF Valentines Celebration in February of 2012. It was a huge success. The women who were present were surprised to learn of the loss of my husband. Most of the women were present at our fourth BFF event and knew of Danielle's passing. They were moved with compassion when I informed them that my husband passed three months prior to this event. They marveled at my strength and resilience to bounce back soon enough to put on this event.

I gave all honor and glory to God and told them, "I don't look like all I've been through." God is definitely a keeper. He is able to keep you when you can't or won't keep yourself. I had to realize that God was keeping me around for a very special purpose, known only to me in part at the time. One thing is for sure, the pain of this second round was by no means over. It would take a miracle from God to heal the deep wounds of this loss. In a few short weeks, I would learn that God had some requirements that I would have to meet before He would allow me to return to ministry on a whole new level. He would begin to tell me that it's not business as usual. All of His promises are true, but they always come with, "If you will do, then I will do . . . !" In other words, there is an obedience clause that must be followed before God begins to bring us into our assignment and purpose. In the next chapter, I will reveal what that instruction of obedience entailed.

STORM CHASER

Don't forget to say your prayers when . . .

God is speaking to you in that still small voice! You know there are some weaknesses that you need to correct in your life, but you muffle the voice of God and keep right on acting as if you did not hear Him.

Sometimes people stop praying and completely shut God out. When trouble comes, when all hell is breaking out on the right and on the left, we grow weary and don't want to hear from anybody including God. We just want to be left alone to figure out how we are going to get through this storm. We just want to ride the waves of the storm in our own boat, hoping that somehow the waves and the wind will settle down and we can then use our oars to make it back to shore.

But even in the midst of the storm God still speaks. Even in the midst of your storm, God still requires obedience. Though He knows your heart is aching from the losses that you have endured, He still has His hands on you, and He still knows the way that you take. God still, through his mercy and grace, is able to bring you boat to safe harbor.

Here are some Scriptures on hearing and obeying the voice of God speaking to you, in the midst of your storm.

Job 33:19 (AMP) *"[God's voice may be heard by man] when he is chastened with pain upon his bed and with continual strife in his bones {or} while all his bones are firmly set."*

Deuteronomy 4:30 (ESV) "*When you are in tribulation and all these things come upon you, in the latter days you will turn to the Lord your God and be obedient to His voice.*"

Numbers 23:19 (NIV) "*God is not a man, that he should lie, nor a son of man, that he should change his mind. Does he speak and then not act? Does he promise and not fulfill?"*

2 Corinthians 10:3–5 (NIV) *"For though we live in the world, we do not wage war as the world does. The weapons we fight with are not the weapons of the world. On the contrary, they have divine power to demolish strongholds. We demolish arguments and every pretension that sets itself up against the knowledge of God, and we take captive every thought to make it obedient to Christ."*

1 Samuel 15:22 (NIV) "*Does the Lord delight in burnt offerings . . . as much as in obeying the voice of the Lord? To obey is better than sacrifice . . . .*"

Zechariah 7:11-13 (NIV) "*But they refused to pay attention; stubbornly they turned their backs and stopped up their ears. They made their hearts as hard as flint and would not listen... So the Lord Almighty was very angry. 'When I called, they did not listen; so when they called, I would not listen,' says the Lord Almighty.'*"

Isaiah 30:20-21 (NIV) "*Although the Lord gives you the bread of adversity and the water of affliction, your teachers will be hidden no more; with your own eyes you will see them. Whether you turn to the right or to the left, your ears will hear a voice behind you, saying, "This is the way; walk in it.*"

John 10:2-5 (NIV) "*The man who enters by the gate is the shepherd of his sheep. The watchman opens the gate for him, and the sheep listen to his voice. He calls his own sheep by name and leads them out. When he has brought out all his own, he goes on ahead of them, and his sheep follow him because they know his voice. But they will never follow a stranger; in fact, they will run away from him because they do not recognize a stranger's voice.*"

STORM CHASING REFLECTIONS

(This space is provided for you to reflect on how you can apply what you've read)

CHAPTER SIX

LYDIA, DO YOU HEAR ME NOW?

Sometimes when we just want to do something and don't know exactly what to do, our inclination is to return to the things that are most familiar. However, the Bible says in Isaiah 43:19, "Behold, I will do a new thing; now it shall spring forth; shall ye not know it? I will even make a way in the wilderness, and rivers in the desert." It is important as children of God that we keep abreast of what God is currently doing or saying to us. We get stuck in familiarity and in the comfort of our environment. We don't embrace newness. We keep the same friends, vacation at the same places, wear clothes that we have outgrown, cook and eat the same foods week after week and the list goes on and on. But the problem with staying with the old and not embracing the new is this:

God has already left the building! He has moved on to the next thing. Yet we are comfortable being in a building that is falling apart; the ceiling is leaking, paper coming off the walls; the furnace has stopped putting out heat; the furniture is outdated, and the moths have destroyed the rest.

I don't know about you, but I do not want to be somewhere if God is not there. Moses told God, and I paraphrase, "God if you don't go with us, I am not going. I cannot lead these people if your presence is not with or among us." Saints, it is dangerous to find yourself in a place that God has left.

At or around the middle of January of 2012, things began to settle down. The reality of Tom's and Danielle's death had sunk in, and life was beginning to reshape itself. The roof had been repaired, and the work in the basement was complete. I had installed an alarm system that would provide some security and comfort that I needed. I took off several weeks from the church. Going back to church to face some of the people and men whom Tom served with on the Deacon board was at times a challenge. People were still a bit uncomfortable. They didn't know how to approach me, or know what to say to me. Some were even a bit disturbed and upset because I did not tell them the seriousness of his illness; his death was a complete shock to most of them.

You can't imagine the shock that I experienced when my pastor gave me the news that he would be going into the hospital for bypass heart surgery. He told the ministers first, and then he shared the information with the congregation. He called each minister personally and told them that he needed their cooperation and support. The surgery and rehabilitation would result in him being away from six to eight weeks. Each of the ministers was assigned a Sunday to preach on a rotating basis. Since there were so many of us, each minister would more than likely have to preach once.

I was the first minister scheduled to preach. I believe I preached on the last Sunday in January of 2012. During my pastor's absence, I thought there would be some jockeying for leadership among the preachers. Who would be in charge? Who would get the most face time in the microphone? Who would Pastor appoint to be in charge of the pulpit? To all of our surprise, it was the chairman of the Deacon Board who was in charge of the church's day to day issues. Our only job as associates was to show up on our assigned Sunday, lead the worship service, preach and sit down.

I thought that I was the person with the most experience in leadership, so maybe Pastor would put me in charge of keeping the other associate ministers apprised of what his wishes. I thought that this was my opportunity to exercise my pastoral calling gift. Was I wrong! I felt this was my opportunity to be used and to show I had matured and had what it took to be an assistant to the pastor. Boy was I delusional!

I finally got my head on straight and realized that would not be the case. If fact, when I mounted the podium on the fourth Sunday in January of 2012, the Holy Ghost whispered in my ear, “This will be your last Sunday because I am ready to move you out of here now.” This had happened before I opened my mouth to give the Word that God had given me to preach. I was devastated and hurt. I couldn’t leave now; my pastor needed me. He depended on me and the other ministers to carry on while he was recuperating from heart surgery.

On several occasions, I was ready to pack up and leave my church, but God would not allow me to do so. Now when I was in the position (I thought) to make some headway in ministry, God gave the instruction that it was time to leave. I should not have been surprised, however. At Tom’s funeral, my pastor gave me a prophetic word. In a nutshell, he told me that God was ready for me to move into the things that He had prepared for me. He said I needed to hold fast the confession of my faith and be faithful to my calling; however, I was not ready to hear that at the moment.

I kept going to church and performing my regular duties, but I could feel God tugging at my heart and urging me to leave my church. I ignored Him. It seemed every word I heard from the pastors, bishops on television and in person, had something to do with walking in your calling, and leaving your comfort zone, getting out of the nest and sprouting wings to soar into your destiny. I could not rest. Finally around late February, I made an appointment to talk with my pastor. He wasn't back to preaching, but he was open to office visits and short meetings.

During that visit, I reminded him about a prior meeting we had to discuss my call to the office of a pastor. We talked about an hour and agreed and disagreed on the method of my leaving to pursue my calling. I had already sent my letter of termination based upon what I knew God was saying in my spirit. My pastor's counsel was for me to wait, think things through and take a sabbatical through the end of the year. So that is what I did. I changed my letter and instead of terminating my membership, I decided to take a sabbatical.

When I left the office, I did not have a sense of peace. Something kept gnawing at my insides. During the weeks that followed, I just did not have a sense of peace and knowing that I had made the right decision. Around March, I decided to rescind my letter, and I made up my mind to obey God. I tendered my resignation letter, making it short and sweet and to the point. I was done, "It is finished!" A sense of peace came over me, and I knew I had heard God right the first time. Obedience is better than sacrifice, The Bible says, "The steps of a good man are ordered by the Lord." (Psalms 37:23 KJV)

Sometimes we get stuck in familiarity, and we don't want to get out of our comfort zone. But like the mother eagle that stirs up her nest and makes it uncomfortable for the little eaglets, until they have no other option but to get out, spread their wings and fly; we too must do that very same thing. Joyce Meyers always encourages people to "do what God tells you to do, even if you do it afraid." We have to remember that God hasn't given us the spirit of fear, but of power, love, and a sound mind." We will miss what God has for us unless we are willing to obey Him completely. Some of us think the opposite of faith is unbelief, when really the antithesis of faith is disobedience. God expects us to be completely upfront and honest with Him. It is okay to share our doubts, fears and concerns with Him. But after we do, He expects us to get up and follow His instructions. There is no such thing as being a little bit pregnant. You are either pregnant or you are not. You are either obedient children of God, or you are not!

I thought my plan would take me to my next level of ministry; however, my motives were completely wrong and messed up. God knew the way to my purpose would still be by way of the wounds of disapproval, rejection, abandonment, loss and grief. He was getting ready to open up my spirit to the real truth about Lydia P. Ford. He was about to uncover or expose me in a way that I had been deceived in my own heart, and it wasn't going to be pretty.

Not only had God spoken to me about leaving my home church, he had been speaking to me about leaving my place of employment for a couple of years. This would be the year when I would have to choose to obey God completely or go back to living beneath my privileges as a daughter of the Most High God. Year after year my classes of students had become more challenging. I thought to myself, "There is no way I can retire now that Tom is gone. He was supposed to be around to continue working and support me in my retirement." After all, I had worked consistently for 35 years in my field of education. It wasn't fair that I would have to support myself and take care of the responsibilities of a house and all the other expenses. I felt I was between a rock and a hard place. I was bitter and angry with Tom, my pastor, my principal, and God. There were others too, but these were primarily the individuals whom I felt made my life difficult in the past, and were making my life difficult in the present.

There was unforgiveness in my heart, and God would have me to take a long and serious look at the condition of my heart. He was not going to allow me to go any further in my calling unless I addressed these serious issues. Yes, we fail to realize that we can get to a place where the Lord plants a speed bump ahead and He forces you to slow down before you approach this next place. Someone once said, "A word to the wise is sufficient."

One night I decided to take a look at a DVD of my last sermon I preached at Hopewell. I was in bed while I watched it. I thought I was doing a fairly good job. The sermon was entitled: "I'm Grown, I Can Speak for Myself" (John Chapter 9:1-12). While I was viewing the DVD, the Holy Ghost said to me, "Yes, you are preaching good, but you are angry, and I will not allow you to continue to preach under those conditions. You must deal with your anger issues." Those words startled me, and I, of course, was in denial. I ignored the Lord and continued on my merry way for several more months.

However, the school situation grew worse. There were a few students who were very challenging. I was still bleeding inside and every day I went to work a broken and hurt woman. I took some of my frustrations out on the children. I did and said things to them that I regretted deeply. I got into a situation with a student and a parent that could permanently scar my teaching career. I wound up downtown at the Board of Education having to answer to some accusations, most of which were lies, but yet a bit of truth was in those statements from the child and the parent.

It was the grace of God that saved me from this assassination plot on my character. The devil thought he would put a black mark on my career as a teacher, but God blocked it and would not let the devil expose me completely. The charges were dropped, and I was exonerated. I learned a very valuable lesson by going through this process. When God shows and reveals your flaws to you, admit them. Do not be in denial; God knows what is in the heart. We don't know what is in our own heart. It is deceitfully wicked! I had to repent before God and admit I had a problem with anger, bitterness and unforgiveness.

God had told me to go and get some help for these issues, but I had failed to do so. Then He had to put me on "Blast" to get my attention. There was a woman of God, who I met at the BFF. My neighbor Bettye told me about her. She was a member of her church, and she was a social worker and counselor. Bettye introduced her to me at the BFF, and I also ran into her at their conference of April 2012. I spoke to her and told her that I would be in touch with her to set up an appointment. But weeks passed, and I had not done what the Spirit of the Lord had told me to do. It wasn't until June of 2012 that I started my counseling sessions at Wellsprings Counseling Center. Minister Syrette helped pave the way for my recovery. But it was solely up to me to recognize that I was sick, and I needed not just a bandage, but I needed to be completely whole. God would not accept a surface healing. He wanted to heal me from the inside out. The Word says, "Jesus learned obedience from the things he suffered." I would have to travel that same road. I would have to know that the way to your next level or dimension is by way of the cross. Nobody wants to hear those words in the Body of Christ, but they are nonetheless true.

I praise God for the surgery that I received in the spirit. The cleansing power of the Lord can root out, pluck up, and cast out every demonic spirit that tries to harass and keep the stronghold that binds us and stifle the anointing that God wants to bless us with. But thanks be to God, who always causes us to triumph in Christ Jesus our Lord.

Often we ask God to speak to us, only to hear back, "if you are so interested in what I think, then why didn't you do the last thing I told you?" Obedience is the response that keeps the dialog going. If we refuse to do what God tells us in the little things, we risk deafening our spiritual ear. If we refuse to do what God speaks in the big things, we risk his active rebuke.

Affirm over your life that whatever the Lord tells you to do, you will do it. If he said it, will he not make it good? God cannot lie.

STORM CHASER

Don't Forget to Say Your Prayers when . . .

You know you are out of the will of God and fear and intimidation has blinded you to the truth. You must get a heart checkup. Sometimes we don't know what is in our own heart. The heart is deceitfully wicked, who can know it but God. You must pray and continue to seek God's direction. We cannot trust people to always tell us the truth! People are often blinded to their own needs and agendas. They cannot and often will not validate what is really going on as you wrestle sometimes with them and God, concerning your assignment and purpose.

When you have doubts and fear of your future pray these Scriptures to get the relief and help you need. They will provide clarity, peace and assurance that God is still with you. He never leaves the scene of the accident. He will send you the help that you need so that you can recover from your misdeeds.

(Psalm 23:4) *"Even though I walk through the valley of death, I will fear no evil."*

Psalm 27:1 (NIV) *"The Lord is my light and my salvation, whom shall I fear?"*

Psalm 46:1-3 (KJV) *"God is my refuge and strength, a very present help in trouble. Therefore will not we fear, though the earth be removed and thought the mountains be carried into the midst of the sea; though the waters thereof roar and be troubled, thought the mountains shake with the swelling thereof, Selah."*

Psalm 55:22 (NASB) *"Cast your burden upon the Lord and He will sustain you; He will never allow the righteous to be shaken."*

Psalm 118:5–6 (KJV) *"I called upon the Lord in distress: The Lord answered me, and set me in a large place. The Lord is on my side, I will not fear: what can man do unto me."*

Proverbs 29:5 (KJV) *"The fear of man brings a snare: But whoso puts his trust in the Lord shall be safe."*

John 14:27 (KJV) *"Peace I leave with you, my peace I give unto you: not as the world gives, give I unto you. Let not your heart be troubled, neither let it be afraid."*

STORM CHASING REFLECTIONS

(This space is provided for you to reflect on how you can apply what you've read)

CHAPTER SEVEN

STRESS, INTIMIDATION, SCARE TACTICS, FEAR, FOLK AND FOOLISHNESS

From the very beginning of time, Satan has sought to destroy Jesus. His goal is and has always been to harass, kill, steal, and destroy the children of God and their destiny. He is the ultimate deceiver, a liar from the beginning of time. His entire purpose is to frustrate the purpose and plans that God has for the life of believers.

In Chapter four of the Book of Ezra, we see how the enemy tried to frustrate the building project that the returning exiles began on the temple of God. The enemy sent stress, unrest, trouble, folk and foolishness in an effort to stop the people from rebuilding the temple. For approximately 16 years, the building of the temple ceased.

Some enemies of the Jews tried to infiltrate the workforce and stop the building with political pressure. Fear caused the work to grind to a halt. The people abandoned the work of God, settled into the comfort of their own homes and went back to their business as usual!

I've been preaching and teaching on spiritual warfare. The bottom line is this: if you want your spiritual inheritance, you're going to have to wage warfare to obtain it. God's plan and purpose for your life are usually not a secret to your haters. Remember, haters see what God is about to do in your life before you do. To reach your destiny or complete the assignment God has for you, you must endure hardness like a good soldier. You have to put on your armor like a soldier puts on his or her uniform.

Fighting for your purpose brings on stress. Stress makes your chest feel tight. Too much stress in your life will cause sickness and disease to set itself up in your body. It is the cause of high blood pressure, high cholesterol, cancer, stomach ailments, anxiety attacks, and so forth. Stress makes things feel tight. Some of you are in a tight place. It's not just one thing that is out of control; it's everything! My friend has an acronym that he uses when negative circumstances keep popping up repeatedly in life. He refers to it as: "ODTAA" (One Damn Thing After Another).

I have found that statement to be the truth! Listen, stress brings trouble, and then trouble brings on unrest and worry, and unrest brings folk to the table. And finally folk brings foolishness into the equation. If the enemy can't get you with any of these factors, he'll try to get you to compromise your position.

In Ezra 4:2, the enemies of the Jews asked to collaborate with them in rebuilding the Temple. But the Jews would have no part in that. The explanation to them was: "We worship the same God you do, and we have sacrificed to him ever since the king of Assyria brought us here."

Well, if that was the case, where were these people when the building project began? Why didn't they help from the very beginning? Folks are a mess! They won't get behind you at the beginning when the struggle is the greatest. They just want to come on board in the middle or towards the end when most of the work has already been completed. Then they want to take some of the credit, if not all the credit for your success.

Then they (referred to as "the adversaries of Judah and Benjamin in Ezra 4:2) said, "We serve the same God you do." Well, that might have been the case, but the truth is they served other gods or idols too. The Book of the Law says: "Thou shall have no other gods before me." God is a jealous God. Serving other gods is the reason why the Jews had been dispersed into enemy camps in the first place.

Next, they tried to brag about the sacrifices they had made. Well, maybe they did make sacrifices, but some held back their sacrifice at the beginning of the temple project. It's no different today. Some people hold back their service because they want to make sure that their investment is a sure thing; they want to make sure that the project will come into manifestation. Some people sacrifice out of their abundance. They have so much that what little they give isn't really a sacrifice to them by a long shot. A sacrifice should cost you something; a sacrifice should be meaningful to you. Consider these New Testament examples:

- The widow who gave her only two mites (Luke 21:1–4)
- Mary of Bethany, who broke her alabaster box and washed Jesus's feet (John 12:2–3)
- The Apostle Paul, who experienced serious misfortunes to take the Gospel to the Gentiles
- Jesus, the Son of God, King of Kings and Lord of Lords, who sacrificed his life for sinful man

Again, a sacrifice should cost you something!

The enemy will try to get you to compromise your beliefs. In fact, the enemy will try to make you believe that everyone is on the same page. But the Bible says to be careful of the leaven of the Pharisees. People sometimes don't know what is in their own heart. They mean well, but often the methods they use to distract and highjack your destiny involves intimidation, manipulation, and domination. You just have to know the Word and voice of God. You must seek His counsel on everything. If He leads you to obtain counsel from another individual, make sure it is someone who you know is mature in the things of God. Make sure you know they hear from God and have a track record of testimonies on how God has moved in their life. Just before your breakthrough, it is imperative that you not be driven by your emotions, or by what you see, think, believe, or feel.

When I finally obeyed God and sought counseling, I was afraid. I felt that my seeking help meant that I was weak. I had let circumstances get out of control, and I felt like a failure. Being in control of the events in my life was paramount to me. Reliance on my faith, abilities, intelligence, resources, friends, and influence were the guiding principles I used to make it through life's problems. But with all of that going on for me, I still was messed up, jacked up, tore up from the floor up; I was a train wreck waiting to happen.

I was in denial of the deep dark pit of despair that I was in. I felt that with time, everything would be back to normal. "Normal" meant I could go back to teaching Sunday school, training new disciples, and preaching in the convalescent homes. "Normal" meant restarting my women's support group, and preaching when asked to do so by my pastor. However, God had a new normal for me. He wanted me to know I would have no peace until I dealt with my anger, bitterness and unforgiveness. Having been exposed, I had no choice but to seek counseling. My counseling sessions began sometime in May or June 2012. As a matter of fact, I am still getting counseling, but on a limited schedule. Praise the Lord!

For 28 years, I was a member of Hopewell, and leaving that church was one of the hardest things I have ever done. I had been a member of the Baptist faith for over 45 years. I was afraid. I knew that God was separating me to the office of a pastor. I knew He wanted me to go into full-time ministry. But none of this made sense to me then. It just didn't add up. My full-time salary barely provided enough to meet my needs, so naturally I wondered how I could go into full-time ministry on a part-time salary.

I had already sought the counsel of my pastor. He offered his help in terms of mentorship once I was certain that God had called me into the office of a pastor. However, I wasn't certain I wanted to remain in the Baptist denomination. I felt that God was calling me to establish a church and this church would be non-denominational.

We did not agree on some things I had hoped we would. We discussed the positive and negatives that would result in my leaving the Baptist denomination.

With respect to my preaching credentials, there are certain rules that stipulated that I may have to turn in my license and ordination certificate if I left the Baptist faith. That created a lot of fear and intimidation. I also became angry because I didn't agree or see the point in turning in my certificates. It was God who called me, not man. I felt I should be free to keep my license and do whatever God was directing me to do and to go wherever God was directing me to go. I left that meeting feeling hurt, angry, dejected and humiliated.

What was he thinking, I thought to myself? He was my spiritual father. He was supposed to care for me spiritually and provide the counsel I needed to go forth into this unknown territory. I loved my pastor, but for the life of me, I did not understand him. Still, I continued to pray for him and trusted God to open the eyes of his understanding. It was difficult, but I was determined not to hold a grudge or continue to let the spirit of offense hold me captive. That was the bait that Satan hoped to keep me tied up so I would give up and go back into my cave of depression. I'm happy to say my spiritual father and I have a very good relationship because we worked at it. God's Agape love helped us to penetrate the walls we both had built up during this time of transition.

However, upon leaving the nest, I thought I was smart and ahead of the game. My little pea-sized brain was always at work. I had spoken to a pastor back in February who was crusading to invite some pastors and some churches in New England to become partners in the Full Gospel Fellowship Ministry, under the leadership of Bishop Paul S. Morton. I had gone to the presentation at one of the area churches, and I was interested in hearing all about it. The Overseer did a convincing job in her presentation, and the fact that she was a woman was a bonus since most times a woman is usually not the one selected to go on a recruiting campaign to bring in other interested parties.

I took an application home and prayed about what the Lord would have me to do. Months had gone by before I contacted this individual. Actually, I think she contacted me first. I finally found the place where she held her worship services and visited for a few Sundays. I also visited other churches after my resignation from my former church. I believe all God wanted me to do during this hiatus was to rest and visit churches. But I was hardheaded and did not listen. I had my own agenda. I wanted to exercise my gifts, and I was determined to get back into the game.

The pastor was wonderful. She was a little different from most pastors I have known. First of all, she was a woman, and I did not know very many women who pastored their own church. She allowed me to come in and immediately put me to work. It was a small church, so there was much work to do. This pastor was getting ready to have a very important conference in this area. This was an opportunity for me to help this event become a success. I was all for that, so I was willing to put my gifts and talents to use.

After a few weeks, I joined the church under the Watchcare Ministry. But shortly thereafter, the pastor started talking to me about some positions that I felt would help to get me where I wanted to be in ministry. I pondered them and told her which one I wanted, and she sent my name to the appropriate office. You have to be so careful when you are out of the will of God. You must make sure you are hearing from God. We get distracted by fear, intimidation, and our own deceitful heart and end up operating in the flesh to get what we want from man. And if we can't get the right man or woman to give us what we want, we will just keep trying different things until we are successful.

After eight weeks or so, the pastor saw fit to ordain me as an elder in the church that I was supposed to only be sitting in, and helping the ministry here and there. During the entire ordination process, I felt uneasy; I wanted her to stop talking, and I wanted her to call it off. I wanted to say to her, "Stop, I can't go through with this," but I kept silent and let her finish. I did not feel relieved or proud of myself. I felt more stress and unrest now because I was certain God's instructions did not include being ordained as an elder in this church. I was already an elder in God's eyes; He was telling me it was time to go to the next level. He had made me a "Pastor," but I had gotten out of position on this one. I did not hear from heaven. This was Lydia's thing all the way.

So here we have it: fear, intimidation, manipulation, stress and unrest, all the ingredients that lead to deception. How in the world would I get out of this one? There is one thing I know about God, He sits high, but He looks low. He will never leave you permanently in a place that is not connected to your destiny. There is always a way of escape if you are willing to accept and take it. That is why you have to keep on praying and keep on seeking the face of God! Never give up. Repent, tell God, "I'm sorry," and go another way.

Well, I found myself sitting in a church service in Middletown. A prophetess and her son (a prophet) had been doing a service for a friend of my pastor. The young man preached and then began to prophesy to several people. The church was small and the altar helpers were few, so I decided to get up and help. I was there with one of the elders from my church along with my pastor. After the prophet had finished, I heard a voice say, "Stand up woman of God." I had taken my seat after the altar work was completed, and I had my head down, so I did not know he was talking to me. The truth is I did not want him to prophesy to me. I was trying to shut my spirit down so nothing would be revealed to him concerning me. Well, that did not work. I stood up, and he began to prophesy.

He actually started by saying, "God just wants to ask you one question, Woman of God. He wants to know when will you start pastoring"? I wanted to crawl under the chair. "No, God didn't just call me out and expose me like that," I thought to myself, and He did it right in front of my pastor. She was sitting on my left, and the other elder was seated on my right. I was embarrassed and ashamed. Why did I leave myself open like that? Why did I put my pastor through all of this drama? I wasn't completely in the wrong, I thought to myself. Surely the pastor could discern who I really was. I believe she knew I was a pastor, but sometimes our own needs blind us to the things God is showing us. God put me on BLAST! I couldn't hide from Him or people anymore. I came to my senses and began to pray and seek His guidance. I needed Him to get me out of the jam that I had gotten myself into.

I went to my pastor and told her that I had to start walking in the office of a pastor. I had to tell her I could not stay with her; I had to leave and be about my Father's business. She was disappointed, of course, but she also told me that we cannot listen to people. We must make sure we are hearing from God. It is often amusing that people in leadership will say profound things to us, but they are sometimes unwilling to follow the advice they give others. I left the ministry at the end of September and began a Women's Bible study in my home. That was the beginning of my road to complete obedience to the Lord's commandment to start, "Don't Forget to Say Your Prayers International Worship Center."

After I had begun to step out in faith with fear and trembling, a sense of peace surrounded me. What would follow would be an amazing walk of faith and trust in God. I started with Jesus and I'm going to see what the end is going to be.

STORM CHASER

Don't Forget to Say Your Prayers when . . .

You feel like someone or something has placed you in a basket or some kind of container and sealed it shut with a lead cover. The person or thing that has tried to keep your mouth shut or prevent your light from shining will be defeated, and you will be rescued. When Satan is closing in on you, remember to keep the Word of God, His thoughts and words in your mind and in your heart.

Speak over your life and encourage yourself in the Lord. Know that Almighty God will deliver and rescue you from the snares of the enemy. Sometimes the enemy looks like the person staring back at you in the mirror.

Use these Scriptures to remind yourself that you are God's child. He is your protector, sun and shield. He watches over His Word to perform that which He has promised you. Let these Scriptures below to assure you that we serve a God that can and will rescue, deliver, strengthen and give you peace, as you take flight and journey to the place God is taking you.

Proverbs 18:10 (KJV) *"The name of the Lord is a strong tower, the righteous run into it and they are safe."*

Psalm 91:2–3 (AMP) *"I will say of the Lord, He is my Refuge and my Fortress, my God; on Him I lean and rely, and in Him I [confidently] trust! For [then] He will deliver you from the snare of the fowler and from the deadly pestilence."*

Psalm 56:13 (AMP) *"For You have delivered my life from death, yes, and my feet from falling, that I may walk before God in the light of life and of the living."*

Isaiah 43:13 (AMP) *"Yes, from the time of the first existence of day and from this day forth I am He; and there is no one who can deliver out of My hand. I will work, and who can hinder or reverse it?"*

Psalm 68:20 (AMP) *"God is to us a God of deliverances and salvation; and to God the Lord belongs escape from death [setting us free]."*

Psalm 18:2 (AMP) *"The Lord is my Rock, my Fortress, and my Deliverer; my God, my keen and firm Strength in Whom I will trust and take refuge, my Shield, and the Horn of my salvation, my High Tower."*

Luke 4:18 (AMP*). "The Spirit of the Lord [is] upon Me, because He has anointed Me [the Anointed One, the Messiah] to preach the good news (the Gospel) to the poor; He has sent Me to announce release to the captives and recovery of sight to the blind, to send forth as delivered those who are oppressed [who are downtrodden, bruised, crushed, and broken down by calamity]."*

STORM CHASING REFLECTIONS

(This space is provided for you to reflect on how you can apply what you've read)

CHAPTER EIGHT

BECOMING A WOMAN WITH WINGS

The future is that vast uncharted ocean of the unknown; it holds a multitude of feelings and events. It may be filled with joy or terror, comfort or sorrow, love or unhappiness, purpose or frustration. When you suffer the trauma of losing a close family member, the future may seem cold and distant. Its uncertainties loom over your head like a dark cloud on a stormy day. Oft times I felt like the Psalmist David when he wrote these words: "My heart is in anguish. The terror of death overpowers me, Fear and trembling overwhelm me. I can't stop shaking. Oh, how I wish I had wings like a dove; then I would fly away and rest! I would fly far away to the quiet of the wilderness. How quickly I would escape—far away from this wild storm of hatred." (Psalm 55:4–8 LAB)

There are several songs, poems and hymns that use the imagery of flying, sprouting wings and taking flight to journey to a place that provides the solace, comfort, and perspective needed when life seems so cruel, uncaring, and insensitive to your needs. The suggestion of flying away to be at rest is sometimes associated with loved ones who have died. Those who remain behind sing songs like: "Some glad morning when this life is over, I'll fly away. To a land on God's celestial shore, I'll fly away." Another gospel song talks about having two wings to veil one's face and two wings to fly away. It seems that mankind longs to escape the vicissitudes of life to draw nearer to the Lord.

The older I get the more I understand that this world is not my home! I am just a pilgrim passing through. I brought nothing into this world, and I will take nothing from it when I leave. This world is becoming more and more wicked, and driven towards a catastrophe end. Sin is more pervasive in the land, and the essence of it is broadcast in living color on every social network available to man. The heart of the people is waxing cold.

Those of us, who are trying to live a Christian life, suffer the same atrocities as the unsaved, because the Bible says, "Time and chance happen to all men." Sometimes stuff just happens, and it happens to good people, too! It was no different in ancient times. In the Old Testament, God sent his messengers: Elijah, Elisha, Isaiah, Jeremiah, Ezekiel, Hosea, and Amos to stand with scores of others who faithfully delivered His message despite rejection, ridicule, and persecution. At times, they were given prophetic visions foretelling coming events.

Nestled near the end of the Old Testament, among what are known as the "minor prophets," is the book of Zechariah. As one of the three post-exilic prophets, along with Haggai and Malachi, Zechariah ministered to the small remnant of Jews who had returned to Judah to rebuild the Temple and their nation. Zechariah encouraged the people to finish rebuilding the Temple, but his message went far beyond those physical walls and contemporary issues. The Lord used Zechariah, giving him apocalyptic imagery and graphic detail. He told of the Messiah, the one whom God would send to rescue his people and to reign over all the earth.

One specific detail caught my attention in Chapter 5. Zechariah sees a vision of a woman in a basket. She represents the wickedness of the nations. There was an angel who packed the woman into a basket. The basket was an ephod, which is a bushel container that held grain. In the vision, the ephod represents an unbalanced weight, which the Jews used to cheat people through the land. This woman is the personification of wickedness. In the text, the woman tries to escape, but the angel places a lead lid firmly over the mouth of the basket.

In verse 9 of chapter 5, two women, representing agents of God carry the basket away to the country of Babylon. The fact that it was being carried away to this particular land is significant because Babylon became a symbol for the center of world idolatry and wickedness. This woman was a picture to Zechariah that wickedness and sin would be taken away from Israel and one day sin would be removed from the entire earth. When Christ died, He removed sin's power and penalty. When we trust Christ to forgive us, He removes the penalty of sin and gives us the power to overcome sin in our life. When Christ returns, He will remove all sin from the earth, allowing people to live in eternal safety and security.

This image of a woman being squeezed into a basket and taken away is quite disturbing. This imagery in Zechariah makes me a bit nervous, because this picture is one that seems to be oppressive and restrictive. The woman in the basket is prevented from escaping. She is in tight quarters, and the lead stopper is too heavy for her to move. I am sure many of you have heard the term referring to someone as "a basket case," meaning the individual is not very bright, is crazy, irresponsible, and sinful. To be in a basket, my sisters and my brothers, can be debilitating, frustrating, and discouraging. One feels hopeless. In a manner of speaking, we're all basket cases!

However, we should not be kept silent and placed in a container with lead on it to keep us stuck in our sins and afflictions. The Bible says, "Whom the Son has set free, is free indeed." This scripture illustrates Jesus' stance on the "basket cases." He doesn't confine us, put us in a box, silence us, or turn and run from us. He confronts us through the Word, showing us that we can decide to change direction, turn from wickedness, and be transformed into a new creation.

The text clearly describes the assailant as a woman who represents "wickedness." Why must it be a female who is characterized as evil or wicked? After all, you didn't hear one woman's name mentioned as being the author or leader of the economic mayhem that this country went through during the fiasco that took place under George Bush's administration. The Republicans, not the Democrats were responsible for the government shut down in the fall of 2013. You didn't hear one woman's name mentioned in the economic catastrophe following President George Bush Jr.'s tenure. The person behind the Enron scandal was a male. The monies paid to AIG after the federal bailout, the corporate mismanagement in the auto industry, the havoc on Wall Street, the torture of the detainees at Guantanamo Bay, and the rise of the right-wing Tea-party leadership all have male leadership at the helm. And most sorrowfully, need I mention perpetrator(s) perpetrator(s of the sinful, shameful acts against young boys, and in some cases girls were found to be of the male gender. Happy and sad to say ladies, we owe much of the debauchery, evil doing, political anarchy, and economic mayhem to the male gender. Now, if that sounds like a little like male bashing, the truth is still the truth! But give this read a few more minutes and all the men that I turn off from reading this chapter, I'll bring them back in before this chapter ends. No doubt there are some pretty evil, wicked women whom we could point to in our history that fit the role as does this woman in Chapter 5. Jezebel and Delilah are two Biblical characters that come to mind. Susan Smith was convicted of the drowning of her two young children, and Casey Anthony was implicated, but not convicted in the death of her daughter.

The Scripture describes the woman trying to get out of the basket and the angel pushing her back in. This picture portrays the fact that God hates sin, and it must be eradicated from our midst. We cannot allow it to run wild and get out of control. It cannot get a grip on us. It must be stifled. Additionally, the symbolism of the woman in the basket has implications for those of us who are trying to live godly in an ungodly world. Many of us are doing the work of the Lord, but we are coming under attack! There are people in our families, church, and inner circle that oppose the plan and purpose God has for our lives. We have an anointing from the Holy One, but the devil wants to keep the oil from flowing. He uses people, power, influence titles and positions, to thwart the assignment of God. The church uses tradition, manipulation, witchcraft and positions to make us "basket cases" and to keep us that way.

The Word says, "Your gift will make room for you"; however, sometimes it seems like it is making room for everybody but you and me. What do you do when you are called to do a work for the Lord, and every window and door seem to be closed in your face? The old folks use to sing a song that says, "Serving the Lord will pay off after a while." It is difficult to serve God when all you've done is try to be the best servant of God you can be. With that said, I believe this text serves both men and women well. God has no respect of person. When the righteous cry out for forgiveness and mercy, remember this: God will deliver them out of the clutches of Satan's hands.

If we were to stop reading the text at verse 8, it would seem there was no help for this woman. But we must read on to verse 9. There are two states of being here. Hallelujah! Yes, there is a woman in the basket; but there are also some women with wings. Zachariah says: "Then I looked up and saw two women coming forward. The wind was in their wings; they had wings like the wings of a stork, and they lifted up the basket between the earth and the sky. Then the angel said, "To the land of Shinar," representing Babylon."

There were some women with wings who lifted up the woman in the basket. They took control of the evilness of sin and carried it off to Babylon. In the new millennium, we won't have to—to use a cliché— "Go to hell in a hand basket!" We won't have to be whisked off and carried off to a land where evil abounds. Sisters, you and I must endeavor to become women with wings. We must strive to become, godly women willing to lift up and carry another sister's burden. Are you saying Pastor Ford, that the strong must bear the infirmities of the weak? Yes, that is what I am suggesting. There are women in baskets all over the world, especially in many third-world countries where women are denied basic rights that men inherit from birth. Women cannot vote, cannot receive an education, are told how many children they can have and in some instances, what the sex of that child must be in order for it to live. Women are being persecuted, sexually exploited, confined to slave labor, and overcome by poverty and illiteracy. Again, you and I must become those godly women with wings so that we can lift and carry our sisters who have been beat down by sin and life's situations.

So Girlfriend, what are the characteristics of a "woman with wings?" We'll, I'm glad you asked!

- When your hope and trust are in God, you're a woman with wings.

- When you don't worry about the opinions of others, you're a woman with wings.
- When you eliminate negative thoughts and people in your life, you're a woman with wings.
- When you overcome evil with good, and let the Lord fight your battles, you're a woman with wings.
- Women with wings are not fearful or weak. They are committed to seeking justice for themselves and other women.
- Women with wings don't tear down other women, but rather speak life into her broken situation.
- Women with wings don't define themselves by their problems, mistakes, or heartbreaks.
- Women with wings are relentless in their fight for total healing, wholeness and restoration.
- Women with wings rise up against pettiness, bitterness, gossip, envy, and strife.
- Women with wings don't become offended when their name is left off the anniversary program or misspelled.
- Women with wings aren't cliquish, rude or petty; they support all ministries of the church.
- Women with wings celebrate the achievements of other women.
- Women with wings don't talk about you when misfortune comes knocking at your door.

These women are able to fly above the perils of this troubled world. They walk by faith and not by sight. They believe they will still bring forth fruit even in their old age.

Zechariah helps us to see *it is the women with wings that we must become.* While both women and men have known basket experiences, we can be delivered! We must refuse to be controlled by our lower nature and controlled by sin and idolatry. We must submit to God, resist the devil, and he must flee. Our faith tells us that because of Jesus' death and resurrection, we cannot be overcome by this ungodly world system. We can fly high like the women in this text because we have the wind of the Holy Spirit beneath our wings. God's Spirit moves us from salvation, deliverance and freedom because The Lord gives us the help we need to fly.

I thank God for the godly men and women whom He placed in my life to undergird me, when I didn't have enough strength to lift up my head, when the tears of sorrow became my pillow every night. Their telephone calls and prays gave me the strength to wipe my weeping eyes. I thank my Lord, who like Paul, I've had to learn obedience through the things that I suffered. David said, "It was good that I was afflicted." It taught him to stand firmly on the Word of God.

I stand here today to say, I never would have made it without the Lord. And now I'm stronger. I'm wiser. I'm better so much better! I'm grateful for the wings that God has given me; they have kept me in the midst of sickness, sorrow, persecution, heartache and disappointment. Women, our wings have helped us to walk by faith and not by sight. When women have wings, we can run and not be weary, we can walk and not faint. We can escape from our enemies and not be swallowed up by our problems. When women have wings, we have healing in our hands, healing that comes because of a regenerated heart and a new spirit. When trouble comes we can fly into the arms of Jesus standing firm in the truth of Philippians 4:13 that we can do all things through Christ, who strengthens us. Fly, my Sister, spread your wings and fly!

STORM CHASER

Don't Forget to Say Your Prayers when . . .

You feel like someone or something has placed you in a basket or some kind of container and sealed it shut with a lead cover. The person or thing that has tried to keep your mouth shut or prevent your light from shining will be defeated, and you will be rescued. Satan is closing in on you, keep the Word of God, His thoughts and words in your mind and in your heart.

Speak over your life and encourage yourself in the Lord. Know that Almighty God will deliver and rescue you from the snares of the enemy. Sometimes the enemy looks like the person staring back at you in the mirror.

Use these Scriptures to remind you that you are God's child. He is your protector, sun and shield. He watches over His Word to perform that which He has promised you. Let these Scriptures below to assure you that we serve a God that can and will rescue, deliver, strengthen and give us peace, as we take flight and journey to the place God is taking us.

Proverbs 18:10 (KJV) *"The name of the Lord is a strong tower, the righteous run into it and they are safe."*

Psalm 91: 2-3 (AMP) *"I will say of the Lord, He is my Refuge and my Fortress, my God; on Him I lean and rely, and in Him I [confidently] trust! For [then] He will deliver you from the snare of the fowler and from the deadly pestilence."*

Psalm 56: 13 (AMP) *"For You have delivered my life from death, yes, and my feet from falling, that I may walk before God in the light of life and of the living."*

Isaiah 43: 13 (AMP) *Yes, from the time of the first existence of day and from this day forth I am He; and there is no one who can deliver out of My hand. I will work, and who can hinder or reverse it?*

Psalm 68: 20 (AMP) *God is to us a God of deliverances and salvation; and to God the Lord belongs escape from death [setting us free].*

Psalm 18: 2 (AMP) *The Lord is my Rock, my Fortress, and my Deliverer; my God, my keen and firm Strength in Whom I will trust and take refuge, my Shield, and the Horn of my salvation, my High Tower.*

Luke 4: 18 (AMP) *The Spirit of the Lord [is] upon Me, because He has anointed Me [the Anointed One, the Messiah] to preach the good news (the Gospel) to the poor; He has sent Me to announce release to the captives and recovery of sight to the blind, to send forth as delivered those who are oppressed [who are downtrodden, bruised, crushed, and broken down by calamity].*

STORM CHASING REFLECTIONS

(This space is provided for you to reflect on how you can apply what you've read)

CHAPTER NINE

GREATER IS COMING

One of my favorite books in the Bible is the Book of Psalms. I particularly love Psalm 27:13. It says, "I would have fainted, unless I had believed to see the goodness of the Lord in the land of the living." I often remind myself, and others that God is going to get the glory out of the things I have suffered. God is not through with me yet. I believe wholeheartedly in heaven. And I know that my reward is going to be great on the other side. But God promised me that if I keep the faith, He will make all things work together for my good right down here. Psalm 92:14 says, "They will still bear fruit in old age; they shall be fat and flourishing." I choose to trust and believe in God's Word.

The gospel singer Jacklyn Carr recently recorded a hit song entitled: "Greater Is Coming." The gospel artist describes in vivid detail the process of being shaped and prepared for greatness. There is a process and there is a price to pay for the anointing that God places upon your life. First, there is a seed sown in the womb of your spirit. God gives you a vision of what you were purposed and destined to be. But then you have obstacles and forces coming against the promise of your dream, vision, or ministry. Many are not willing to go through the process because it cost too much! The cost is sometimes too high a price to pay on your way to meet with destiny. I suppose if God showed us everything we would have to endure, some of us would have waved good-bye a long time ago. There is truth to the statement: "Only the strong survive." We get beat up and beat down on the road to success. Everything in our lives that can be shaken *will be* shaken. Life and chance happen to all men. Tragedies, misfortunes, setbacks, betrayal, sickness, often death of loved ones put your goals on pause, and sometimes bring them to a grinding stop!

To get to the finish line, ladies and gentlemen, we must have the passion and pressing in our spirit to go all the way, regardless of the pain, suffering, negativity and rejection that we encounter along the journey. The Spirit of God puts that drive and perseverance within us to keep us motivated to complete the task and go all the way to fulfillment of our goals. Those who are chosen by God for greatness must have faith and believe God has given them the power to complete and finish what He has started.

Occasionally, I still ponder why God allowed me to go through the pain and suffering of losing Danielle and Tom a year apart and on the same day. I remind myself that the Bible says God's ways and thoughts are not the same as ours. We don't know why He allows us to suffer in this world. But we do know that the Bible says, "If we are to reign with Him, we must also suffer with Him." Suffering covers a wide spectrum of human experiences. My suffering may not be like yours, but we share a common bond since a woman's life is inextricably tied to suffering.

Suffering is an experience of desolation and aloneness. You might feel separated from God, from people, and from the act of living. Suffering is an experience of desperation; it is a longing for life as we once knew it, yet understanding that life will never be the same. Suffering is life threatening. It threatens our souls, our minds, and our hearts. The disappointments and disillusionment of life poison our thinking, our feelings and threaten our ability to live an abundant life.

Hannah and Elizabeth suffered from the emptiness of barrenness. American slaves experienced suffering through slavery. The Jews experienced suffering at the hands of Hitler during the Holocaust. The victims of domestic violence experience suffering at the hand of their abusers. Survivors of the earthquake in Haiti experienced suffering, and the parents who lost their children in the massacre at Sandy Hook School in Connecticut are still living with the tragedy of that horrific event.

Even Jesus experienced suffering during Passion Week leading up to the crucifixion. Although a person may suffer, the sovereignty of God can bring meaning into the worst conditions and situations of that suffering. Suffering causes one to withdraw. We become disheartened as we search for understanding. We question and cry out in great despair only to discover a self we may have not known before—an angry self, a hateful self, a vengeful self, a despondent self, and a longing self. In our suffering, we discover a self who understands that without God, there is no life.

The Bible says that Jesus was a man of sorrow, acquainted with grief. (Isaiah 53:3) That lets us know that He is full of mercy and compassion. We are to take our burdens to the Lord, for His yoke is easy, and His burdens are light. In the Garden of Gethsemane, Jesus understood that unless He died, we would not have life. (Matthew 26:36-46) Jesus said, "I came that you might have life and that you might have it more abundantly." This then is the paradox of life. If the Bible is true that Jesus came to give us life and that more abundantly, why is it that He allows us to experience so much suffering? That is a paradox to many, including Christians!

Preacher, do you mean that I'm supposed to experience the good life while understanding that life can and will yield some terrible blows, tragic events, mind blowing destructive acts that will test and try my soul? Yes, that is what I am saying! Until Jesus' hands and feet were nailed to the cross, until He hung, bled, and died, we would not have been allowed to experience life. His death brought life. He is the "Resurrection and the life." The words of one of my favorite hymns sum it up nicely, "Because He lives, I can face tomorrow, because He lives all fear is gone. Because I know He holds the future, and life is worth the living, just because He lives."

I know that my life has a greater meaning now. Jesus learned obedience through the things He suffered. I had to learn obedience through the things I suffered, and I also learned there is a cost to serving the Lord. The amount of your pain and suffering, I believe, is akin to the depth and power of the anointing you will receive after you have passed the test. Many people trust God when there is smooth sailing, but can and will you trust Him when the storms are raging and the winds and the waves are beating against your ship?

God is looking for a people who will grab a hold of the broken splintered pieces of the boat (their life) and declare: "I'm going to make it to shore (to my destiny), with what I have left. I am not forsaken; God has not abandoned or forgotten me. And after He has tried me, I will come forth as pure gold." Sometimes we have to do like

Jacob did and tell the angel, “I won’t let go until you bless me!”

I don’t always know what God is doing in my life. I know I am not the only one who questions God! But though we might be troubled on every side, we are not distressed; we are perplexed, but not in despair; persecuted, but not forsaken; cast down, but not destroyed; because He lives we are always bearing about in the body the dying of the Lord Jesus that the life also of Jesus might be made manifest in our mortal body. (Romans 8:38-39)

In other words, what happened to Jesus will happen to us. We will go through trials, torture, mocking, sickness, disease, death of loved ones, misfortune, etc. For we who live are always delivered unto death for Jesus's sake. Often we don’t know what to do, but we know that God knows what to do, and He will never leave our side. Though I have been through some rough seas, and the storms of life have battered my ship, I still believe that my greater is coming.

There is a thread, a fiber that maintains a sense of balance between life and suffering. It comes to test to our profession of faith in God through Jesus Christ. It comes as a unique opportunity to glorify God, in the midst of the storm. Our suffering is our testimony that: “I never lost my praise, my hope, or my joy.” Our suffering is a testimony that nothing shall be able to separate us from the love of God, which is in Christ Jesus our Lord. (Romans 8:39 KJV)

Jonathan Nelson sings a song entitled: "There Will Be a Performance." The title is akin to God saying that: "He who has begun a good work in you will be faithful to perform it."(Philippians 1:6). I believe my recovery and transition from my old season to the new season has begun. The Lord is restoring the years that the enemy has stolen from me. The Lord has blessed me with a total of three beautiful granddaughters. My son, Trevor and his wife have two girls: Brianna, 19 months and Brittany 6 months. God has given me more than double for my trouble. He has placed a very good friend in my life for which I am grateful. My ministry has transitioned, and I am now the founding pastor of Don't Forget to Say Your Prayers International Worship Center. And though the ministry is still growing, the Bible says, "Don't despise these small beginnings, for the Lord rejoices to see the work begin. Zechariah 4:10 NLT)

I know and believe that greater is headed my way. I just need to remain steadfast, focused and faithful to what God has promised me. Sometimes we miss God by desiring what other people have, and wanting our ministries to mirror what others look like. But God says your gift will make room for you. He specializes in uniqueness. No two people have the same fingerprints or DNA. God has made me an original; therefore, I must do things exactly as He lays them out for me to do. Romans 5:3 says, “And not only so, but we glory in tribulations also: knowing that tribulation worketh patience; and patience, experience, and experience hope: and hope maketh not ashamed.” The problem is we want the glory without the story. We don’t want to go through anything to get the anointing of God. But God desires to give us an experience so we will have a test to go along with our testimony! No story, no glory! No test, no testimony! No misery, no ministry!

The only wonders in the world are Stevie Wonder and Wonder Bread. If you expect to be a wonder overnight, you are going to be sadly disappointed. Greatness comes when you spend time on the Potter’s Wheel. Greatness comes when you go through the shaking, beating and pressing. To get olive oil, there must be a pressing; the same is true for wine. It is when you are pressed to the point where there is no more of you left that you are ready for promotion. It is when you have no more to give then God steps in and infuses you with His strength. He gives you the grace to do things you thought were impossible. He is just waiting for you to run out of yourself and into His arms.

I stand as a witness that God will heal you and restore you. You will dance again. You will laugh again. You will hope again. Your will love again. I never expected that I would love again, hope again, or dream again, but God has shown me that His love is unlimited. Once He completes His renovation work in us, His love will fill us in our waste places. His love and joy will overflow onto others that we may not have loved or thought we could love on our own. My advice is simple: let go, and watch God do it!

STORM CHASER

Don't Forget to Say Your Prayers when . . .

It feels like your suffering will never come to an end. Sometimes it seems like that cold, dark night will never be over. Often it seems like God's ears are closed to your petitions, requests and desperate prayers. But I need to remind you that God is not moved by your desperation! God is moved by your faith!

You and I must trust God completely. Either we are going to believe the entire Bible or we are not going to believe any of it! We have to learn to stand on it, meditate on it, and speak His Word over our lives and the lives of our loved ones. When you feel tempted to give up, when you feel like your destiny and purpose is lost in a sea of despair, pray these Scriptures over and over.

Philippians 1:6 (NKJV) *" . . . that He who has begun a good work in you will complete it . . . ."*

Romans 5:3 9 (KJV) *" . . . and not only so, but we glory in tribulations also: knowing that tribulation worketh pa-*

tience; And patience, experience and experience hope: and hope maketh not ashamed."

2 Corinthians 4:8–9 (NKJV) *"We are hard-pressed on every side, yet not crushed; we are perplexed, but not in despair; persecuted, but not forsaken; struck down, but not destroyed—always carrying about in the body the dying of the Lord Jesus, that the life of Jesus always may be manifested in our body."*

John 10:10 (NAS) " . . . *I came that they might have life, and might have it abundantly."*

Isaiah 53:3 (KJV) " . . . *a man of sorrow and acquainted with grief."*

Proverbs 3:5–6 (NKJV) *"Trust in the Lord with all your heart and lean not on your own understanding; in all your ways acknowledge him, and he shall direct your path.*

1 John 4:4 (KJV) *"Ye are of God, little children, and have overcome them: because greater is he that is in you than he that is in the world."*

STORM CHASING REFLECTIONS

(This space is provided for you to reflect on how you can apply what you've read)

CHAPTER TEN

THERE IS NO SUBSTITUTION FOR OBEDIENCE

There are several character traits one can use to describe me as a person. But the most notable one as far as I am concerned is *loyal*. I am loyal to my convictions, loyal to my friends and the services which I perform for others. I looked up the word *loyal* in the dictionary and found several meanings. Here are a few of them:

The word *loyal* as defined by the Free Online Dictionary, Thesaurus means: Steadfast in allegiance to one's homeland, government, or sovereign. 2. Faithful to a person, ideal, custom, cause, or duty. 3. Of, relating to, or marked by loyalty.

While being loyal is a wonderful trait to possess, it can also operate to your detriment if you do not also use the spiritual gift of discernment when seeking direction and guidance from God. It is extremely important to know what season you are in. Using discernment will help you know God's timing for changing jobs, churches, ministry, selecting a spouse, building financial security, etc. The trait of loyalty becomes problematic, especially when pleasing your spouse, boss, pastor, ministry and friends supersedes your obedience and loyalty to God.

Disobedience caused God to tear the kingdom away from King Saul and give it to a young shepherd boy named David. Disobedience caused Sampson to lose his anointing, have his eyes gouged out and to be captured by the Philistines. Disobedience to God caused the men Jonah was sailing with to throw him into the sea because they discerned he was the one who brought trouble to their seafaring excursion. Little did Jonah know God had prepared a big fish to open its mouth and swallow him before he hit the water!

So what does that have to do with you and me, you might ask? Several times the Lord spoke to me regarding preparation to starting the church, but I didn't receive it because I was not financially able or ready to retire and do full-time ministry. And frankly speaking, my husband was not that excited about me starting a ministry in our home. Tom resisted the thought of my leaving our church and going somewhere on a number of occasions. He was content where he was and loved the Deacons Ministry. On the other hand, I felt God pushing me out the door, not just at my church, but at my job as well.

Being a loyalist can leave you stuck—lying at the pool like the man in the 5th chapter of John. You can wind up being stuck alongside all the infirmed people in your environment. In fact, you can become so comfortable in that condition until getting up is not even on your mind. If you remain in that condition long enough, your muscles, bones, tendons, etc., don't have the strength to support your body because of paralysis and lack of movement. Consequently, you begin listening to others that are in the same condition as you. You make excuses for why you are stuck, incapacitated and unable to move to another location.

You may be limited financially because you might be stuck in a job with a glass ceiling. You may be stuck relationally because everyone is on the same level as you. No one has any upward thinking; no one thinks out the box; no one can elevate your thinking, so everyone remains stuck waiting for a miracle to happen. You are stuck mentally because, unless you change your mind first, your physical location will remain the same. You have to visualize yourself as victorious. You have to visualize yourself as prosperous in mind, body, and soul. You have to see yourself ministering on the level God has spoken to you in your dreams and/or through His Word. You have to visualize your deliverance from any limitation and the infirmity that keeps you bound to the pool of disobedience and indecision!

Sometimes fear will immobilize you. Fear of the unknown will scare you to death. Many people are not afraid to fail; some are afraid to succeed. I think there are times when I am actually afraid to succeed. It is a bit intimidating to think the Lord desires to take me to a place of unlimited resources and blessings. The point is you and I must be willing to let go of the life we have planned, to have the life God has waiting for us.

During my leave from my home church, I began to ask God for churches to visit until I knew what He wanted me to do next. I stated earlier that I visited a particular church and ultimately joined. However, I never was supposed to join the church, I merely was supposed to fulfill an assignment the Lord sent me on. In retrospect, I realize the assignment had more to do with me and what I wanted than it had to do with God and what He wanted for me.

The pastor was pleasant, welcoming and happy to have some assistance. The longer I stayed, the more I began to feel useful to the ministry. I was fulfilling a role that looked very pastoral to me, and it felt good. Isn't it something how the enemy will dangle a carrot in front of you to trick you into thinking, "This is it! This is what you have been waiting on."? But we have to remember that the devil knows how to bless you too. Things might look favorable, and you may think that the Lord is in this "thing." But look out; it just may be your imagination running away with you. It may be a setup to take you off course. The devil knows the exact areas of stress and rejection you have experienced. He purposely tries to provide delicacies that make you mouth water, and your tongue salivate.

Do you mean I get to be the State Director of Women's Ministry for the entire district? Do you mean I get to travel to conferences up and down the East Coast to minister and give direction to other Women's Ministry groups? Women's Ministry was an area that I had provided leadership in for over ten years or more. Looking at an opportunity to lead a statewide women's ministry organization was enticing and something I did not want to pass up. The position was there for the asking. I told the pastor that I would pray about it and get back to her.

I became engrossed with the possibility of gaining some restitution and notoriety as a State Director of Women's Ministry for the Full Gospel Baptist Fellowship. This was some delicious bait that was dangled in front of me, but the Lord sent a prophet to remind me that He had a different purpose in mind for me. And to be frank with you, I heard the Lord plainly, but I didn't want the job. I saw what pastoring was like up close and personal, and it was not at all attractive to me! Sometimes I am in denial and believe that everybody can hear God except me. Unfortunately, the only thing I had on my mind was seeking a title and position. The position being offered to me would add validation to my ministry, which would legitimize my reasons for leaving my former church and ministry. This word spoken by the prophet was a confirmation from God. I wasn't crazy; I heard God clearly. The gifts and calling of the Lord are without repentance. Remember, whatever God has called you to do, God will bring it to pass. The Bible says, "In all your getting, get understanding."

After God exposed me publicly, I got busy seeking His face as to how to begin this new journey. When the days of my service and help were completed, I called my pastor and told her my assignment was up, and that I had to be about my Father's business. That was not an easy task because this pastor had made it so easy to fit into the ministry and was extremely appreciative of the spiritual gifts and ministry experience I bought to the table. I believe the Lord always speaks to His leaders. It wasn't a real shock that I was called to fulfill the office of a pastor; however, there are times our current needs cloud the vision and the way we should deal with associate ministers and other lay leaders.

The pastor accepted my resignation and bid me God's speed. Things were a little cold at first, but time and the way you leave a ministry heal all wounds. My mom always said you have to be careful how you leave home; you may have to come back again. Having left that ministry, I began to ponder how I was going to prepare for this pastorate. It was clear the Lord was bringing me out from the traditional church. Would I be the founder of a church? That is what I needed God to clarify for me. I decided I would start a Bible study in my home. It would be a women's Bible study because I wasn't open to receiving men in my home just yet. The Bible study started in September of 2012. A few of my friends joined the fellowship and we met every Tuesday evening at 6:30.

Jesus went through some of the same growing and learning pains that we go through, except that He never sinned. This is good news because it means you and I can always go to Him and ask for grace. We can always go to Him to get an understanding of what He desires to do in our lives. We do not have to be clueless, because the Holy Spirit is resident within us to act as our guide and umpire.

Let's look at a portion of Scripture in Hebrews chapter 5, to get more clarity on the comparison that was made between the Old Testament priest, and this New Testament Jesus that is referred to as our, "High Priest. This is the New International Version of this portion of Scripture:

> 1 *Every high priest is selected from among the people and is appointed to represent the people in*

matters related to God, to offer gifts and sacrifices for sins. [2] He is able to deal gently with those who are ignorant and are going astray, since he himself is subject to weakness. [3] This is why he has to offer sacrifices for his own sins, as well as for the sins of the people. [4] And no one takes this honor on himself, but he receives it when called by God, just as Aaron was. [5] In the same way, Christ did not take on himself the glory of becoming a high priest. But God said to him, "You are my Son; today I have become your Father." [6]And he says in another place, "You are a priest forever, in the order of Melchizedek." [7]During the days of Jesus' life on earth, he offered up prayers and petitions with fervent cries and tears to the one who could save him from death, and he was heard because of his reverent submission. [8]Son though he was, he learned obedience from what he suffered [9]and, once made perfect, he became the source of eternal salvation for all who obey him [10]and was designated by God to be high priest in the order of Melchizedek.

It is a mind-blowing thought when we consider Jesus was both human and divine. He entered this world through the womb of a woman just like each of us. Jesus had his earthly parents Mary and Joseph, along with other siblings. His father Joseph was a carpenter by trade, and most likely Jesus learned carpentry skills from him. Jesus was a Jew, and his parents taught him the ways, laws, and statutes of the patriarchs of the Mosaic Law. He observed the Jewish holy days, its feast and holy convocations. Jesus was a son who was obedient to his earthly parents as well as his Heavenly Father.

When we falter and go astray, the hand of the "Great Shepherd," guides us back to safety within the fold. Sometimes He uses the rod gently; then other times He must apply more consistent prodding, tugging and pulling. He uses the Word of God, prophets who are sent by God, ordinary people, trials, what we would call adversaries, circumstances, and time, to get us back into His will.

After I started the Bible study in my home, God reminded me I was only partially fulfilling the assignment He had given me. It wasn't until January of 2013 that the doors of *Don't Forget to Say Your Prayers* church were open. And as the founding pastor, I preached the first sermon to those He sent to be witnesses of its birth.

Every one of us must come to a place of decision for Christ. As witnesses of the grace of Jesus Christ, having been saved from sin and the wrath to come, we must not be afraid to stand firm in our faith as witnesses of His unfailing love and mercy. We must obey God without compromise. We cannot serve God part-time. There is no substitution for disobedience. God is looking for us to walk by faith and not by sight. He desires that we put our confidence and trust in Him. When we do, He promises to lead us to victory, so that we do not succumb to fear and intimidation from the enemies of Christ.

I hope I have given you some insight as to why we must obey God, and not man. Some soul is waiting and depending on you and me to honor God and walk in the purpose and plan that He has for our lives.

STORM CHASER

Don't forget to say your prayers when . . .

Your flesh wants to go running off in the opposite direction of what God has spoken. Remember that the grass always looks greener on the other side. What may look like the perfect scenario may in fact be a trap that derails you from walking into your destiny and divine purpose. It is always profitable to obey God rather than man.

Remember also that although the Lord may send a prophet to prophesy into your life the things that they see in the spirit aforetime, that you too have the Holy Spirit living down on the inside of you. The prophetic word comes along side and confirms what God has already spoken, or has been dealing with you about. We must wait on the timing of God. He makes all things work out in his time. Even when things look slow and forward progress seems to be taking its time like a snail, be faithful in the work God has called you to do.

Read and meditate on the Scriptures daily. They will provide the guiding light and insight to keep a well-lit path for your journey.

Exodus 19:5 (NIV) *"Now if you obey me fully and keep my covenant, then out of all nations you will be my treasured possession. Although the whole earth is mine."*

Deuteronomy 11:1 (NIV) *"Love the LORD your God and keep his requirements, his decrees, his laws and his commands always."*

2 Corinthians 10:5 (NIV) *"We demolish arguments and every pretension that sets itself up against the knowledge of God, and we take captive every thought to make it obedient to Christ."*

Hebrews 13:17 (NIV) *"Obey your leaders and submit to their authority. They keep watch over you as men who must give an account. Obey them so that their work will be a joy, not a burden, for that would be of no advantage to you."*

2 John 1:6 (NIV) *"And this is love: that we walk in obedience to his commands. As you have heard from the beginning, his command is that you walk in love."*

Romans 5:19 (NIV) *"For just as through the disobedience of the one man the many were made sinners, so also through the obedience of the one man the many will be made righteous."*

James 1:25 (NIV) *"But the man who looks intently into the perfect law that gives freedom, and continues to do this, not forgetting what he has heard, but doing it—he will be blessed in what he does."*

STORM CHASING REFLECTIONS

(This space is provided for you to reflect on how you can apply what you've read)

CHAPTER ELEVEN

TAKE THE MEDICINE, GET ON THE COUCH AND GET A HEAD CHECK

It is difficult for most of us in the body of Christ to think we should seek professional help with our issues. We have gotten so saved that we don't refer to them as "sins" anymore. The mere mention of counseling for most men evokes pure denial, pride, and what they feel is an attack or discrediting of their manhood. Most men feel they have an innate ability to solve not only their own problems, but their wives, significant other, and their children's as well.

The responsibility of pastors to attend to their congregants' spiritual and emotional needs is at a critical juncture today. There seems to be as much if not more depression, suicide, physical and emotional abuse in the church as in the secular world. Many now view the role of pastors to include mental health counseling. Additionally, congregants seem to expect it (Stone, 2001). The term *counselor* appears in several Bible verses, such as: "Also Jonathan, David's uncle, was a counselor, a wise man, and a scribe; and Jehiel the son of Hachmoni was with the king's sons" (1 Chronicles 26:14). (Proverbs 11:14) says, "Where no counsel is, the people fall; but in the multitude of counselors there is safety."

The original New Testament Greek word *parakletos*, which literally means "called to one's side," was used to describe someone who helped others by defending or comforting them. In English-language versions of the Bible, *parakletos* is usually translated as advocate, comforter, helper, or counselor (Strong, 2004). It is a term we in church use to describe the third person of the Godhead, namely, the Holy Spirit. But it is also sufficient to say that God has given spiritual gifts to His church. Within the body of Christ, there are pastors, elders, and professional people who are trained psychologists, social workers, and other types of mental health caregivers who can counsel and come alongside a congregate to assist him or her in the journey back to wholeness.

In 1757, Scottish philosopher David Hume wrote that mankind hangs "in perpetual suspense between life and death, health and sickness, plenty and want . . . conditions which are distributed amongst the human species by secret and unknown causes. These unknown causes, then, become the constant object of our hope and fear . . . I am indeed persuaded, that the best and indeed the only method of bringing everyone to a due sense of religion, is by just representations of the misery and wickedness of men" (Hume, 1889).

One of my former pastors used to say, "If you have never experienced any problems, just keep on living." I believe all of us come to a due sense of religion. Sometimes you hear it said that convicts have received, "a jailhouse conversion" or "jailhouse religion." Certainly the experience of being placed behind prison walls, having all your rights taken from you, dealing with the degradation of prison life, being isolated from family and friends, apparently causes many to reach out to God and religion.

Often, we are prisoners in our own homes and bodies. We experience life and chance on a daily basis. No one knows the hour of the day when tragedy, calamity, death, sickness or disease will decide to make a house call to your address or mine.

It is important that Christians begin to search their hearts and ask, "Is Christian Counseling right for me?" Seeking out therapy is an individual choice. There is a myth in the church that people of great faith do not need to seek the help of Christian counseling. There are many reasons why people seek a Christian Counselor: Sometimes it is to deal with long-standing psychological issues that may have not been resolved at the altar on Sunday mornings. At other times, it is in response to unexpected changes in one's life such as the death of a child, parent, spouse, and divorce or work transition. Many seek the advice of a Christian counselor for spiritual guidance as they pursue their own personal exploration and growth.

Working with a Christian counselor can help provide insight, support, and new strategies for all types of life challenges. Counseling along with prayer can help address many types of issues, including depression, anxiety, conflict, grief, stress management, body-image issues, and general life transitions. Christian counseling is right for anyone who is interested in getting the most out of his or her life by taking responsibility, creating greater self-awareness, and working towards positive changes in their lives.

According to the American Association of Pastoral Counselors (AAPC) nearly three-fourth of Americans claim their whole approach to life is based on religion. But I contend that religion alone cannot cure the ills and mental anguish of every believer. There are some Best Practices trained Christian counselors use along with their own spiritual gifts that add more strength and power in the healing and deliverance of an individual. Even Jesus employed some basic practical steps when people came to him for healing. It wasn't all spiritual. He told the lame man to stand up. He told the man with the withered hand to stretch out his hand. He told the boy who was born blind to go and wash in the pool of Siloam. Jesus was both spiritual and practical.

I do not recommend going to a secular counselor. Personally, I preferred to go to counselors who shared my religious (spiritual) beliefs rather than have a therapist who challenged my faith or tried to convert me to some crazy "New-Age Philosophy." Eighty-three percent of Americans believe their spiritual faith is closely tied to their state of mental and emotional health. Three-fourths say it is important for them to see a professional counselor who integrates their values and beliefs into the counseling process.

The counselor who was recommended to me came from a friend whom I highly respected. She knew about the issues surrounding the losses that I had experienced. And as a dear friend, she recognized that I needed professional help mixed with the anointing of a spiritual vessel that God was using to restore people back to wholeness and better mental health.

I asked myself, "Do I really need counseling?" I can usually handle my problems. I felt I was a strong enough person to handle my problems; however, I was in denial! The pain I felt was coming from all different directions. It wasn't just the deaths of Tom and Danielle, there were a lot of messages that my soul and my emotions were receiving based on what was currently going on in my life. But there were a significant number of things in my past that I had not dealt with. All of those memories, the disease, pain, guilt, rejection, and unforgiveness—just to name a few—were things that I did not confront earlier in my life. Those things were now resting in the seat of my soul. My heart was extremely heavy, and my mind was on overload. I could have exploded at any given moment.

Everyone goes through challenging situations in life, and while you may have successfully navigated through other difficulties you've faced, this season of your life might be the time when you have to make the decision to fix your life! There's nothing wrong with seeking out extra support when you need it. In fact, therapy or counseling is for people who have enough self-awareness to realize they need a helping hand, and that is something to be admired. Bringing a spiritual aspect to the counseling sessions can provide comfort and peace that you've not experienced before. Using biblical principles provides you with the assurance that the Holy Spirit is part of the healing process. And I thank God that He showed up in every session!

Some of you may be asking yourselves, "How can Christian Counseling help me?

A number of benefits are available from participating in a faith-based approach to therapy. Many people find the spiritual aspect to be a tremendous asset to managing personal growth, interpersonal relationships, family concerns, and the difficulties of daily life. Counseling can provide a fresh perspective to an overwhelming problem or point you in the direction of a solution. Often you will discover that your current problems are rooted somewhere in your past. The benefits you obtain from counseling depend on how well you use the process and put into practice what you learn.

Counseling can help you learn new ways to deal with stress. It can also help you to understand yourself, your strengths and weaknesses better. Counseling points you in the direction of seeking wholeness, which often means forgiving family members, friends, co-workers and saints who have wronged you. It definitely will address old patterns of behavior and help you to gain new skills to help you achieve success in areas of past failures. The bottom line is this: you want to find the answers to the problems that led you to seek therapy.

In my case, I clearly heard the Holy Spirit tell me I was angry and needed to address that issue before He continued to allow me to preach to His people. This happened one night when I decided to look at a DVD recording of the last sermon I preached at my home church. I thought I was doing a fairly good job with the text but right in the middle of my watching it, the Lord said, "It's good, but you're angry. And that is the spirit that is spewing out all over my people." When I heard those words, a conviction came over me and a feeling that I needed to repent, which I did.

It only was a couple of months since Tom's death, and already the Lord was messing with me! Wasn't it enough that I was almost half crazy from dealing with two deaths so close together? But He knew that He—and a few other people were the objects of this festering anger stirring in my heart.

Unfortunately, I didn't heed the first warning and things intensified at work. In fact, things got so bad at work that I could have been severely disciplined by my employer. I was in a tight situation, but thankfully, by the grace of God everything worked out. After a few close calls, I called the woman of God who would become my counselor and friend. I made the decision to spend the next two years working on becoming whole again.

Sometimes we get so sick that we fear taking the medicine. We feel that we are way beyond help because the illness has persisted for so long. If only we had taken the "medicine" at the beginning, we would be in much better shape! By medicine, of course, I mean counseling. Most people equate counseling with having to lie down on a couch, but that was not the case. But there are times when our physician recommends medication to help us with our emotional and mental anxieties. My physician wrote me out a prescription to help with depression and sleeplessness. I took sleeping pills moderately because there were nights when I tossed and turned all night. Memories of my loved ones stayed on my mind. I kept nursing and rehearsing scenarios, what if this or what if that! A lot of guilt ran through my mind.

Truthfully, sometimes you have to take the medicine for your sanity and the sanity of your family. You should not be ashamed if you need that kind of help or support. However, make sure you take it responsibly. Make sure your family knows what you take and how often you take it. Taking prescription medication doesn't mean you don't trust God or have faith. There are some Christians that won't take radiation or chemo-therapy for the diagnosis of cancer as the treatment recommended by their oncologist. They choose to stand firmly on their faith in God as a healer, yet many die because they refused to get the medical help for the cure that could possibly put them in remission or save their lives. The Bible says, "in all your getting, get an understanding." Improper teaching and training of our congregants are doing more harm than good. All churches should have a health and wellness ministry to provide professional information to the congregations.

The more informed we are, the easier it is to make decisions related to our health and the health of our loved ones. We must be aware of the qualifications of our pastors and leaders. Many do not have the credentials and proper training to address severe mental health issues.

Getting an accurate evaluation and diagnosis is critical to someone's life. Make sure you know the resources that are available in your church. Ask questions. Don't be afraid to take referrals from people you trust. Check into your pastor's credentials to determine if his or her pastoral training is sufficient to meet your needs. Don't feel that you are out of line or hurting your pastor's feelings if the Lord is sending you somewhere else to get help. After all, it is better to be safe than sorry!

Don't forget that the Word of God is powerful! Eat as much of it as you can. Fast, pray, praise and worship your way through, and trust that God will never put more on you than you can bear.

STORM CHASER

Don't forget to say your prayers when . . .

You find yourself between a rock and a hard place. Pray *plus* faith *minus* doubt are great strategies to confront your issues, your demons, your adversary, but sometimes as I have stated, you have to get some counseling, and maybe take the medicine. Here are some helpful Scriptures that deal with the topic of counseling. Enjoy.

Proverbs 13:10 (AMP) *"Only by pride cometh contention: but with the well advised [is] wisdom."*

John 16:13 (AMP) *"Howbeit when he, the Spirit of truth, is come, he will guide you into all truth: for he shall not speak of himself; but whatsoever he shall hear, [that] shall he speak: and he will shew you things to come."*

Proverbs 20:5 (AMP) *"Counsel in the heart of man [is like] deep water; but a man of understanding will draw it out."*

Proverbs 12:18 (AMP) *"There is that speaketh like the piercings of a sword: but the tongue of the wise [is] health."*

2 Timothy 3:16–17 (KJV) *"All scripture is given by inspiration of God, and is profitable for doctrine, for reproof, for correction, for instruction in righteousness: That the man of God may be perfect, thoroughly furnished unto all good works."*

Luke 16:31 (NKJV) *"But he said unto him, 'If they do not hear Moses and the prophets, neither will they be persuaded, though one rise from the dead.'"*

Proverbs 15:22 (KJV) *"Without counsel purposes are disappointed: but in the multitude of counsellors they are established."*

Proverbs 1:1–4 (KJV) *"The proverbs of Solomon the son of David, king of Israel; To know wisdom and instruction; to perceive the words of understanding; To receive the instruction of wisdom, justice, and judgment, and equity; To give prudence to the simple . . . "*

STORM CHASING REFLECTIONS

(This space is provided for you to reflect on how you can apply what you've read)

CHAPTER TWELVE

HE RESTORETH MY SOUL

If I were to rewrite this Scripture: "Come, let us return to the Lord; for he has torn us, that he may heal us; he has struck us down, and he will bind us up" (Hosea 6:1), I would make it ever so personal. "Lord I am coming to You now; for you have torn me, that You may heal me; You have struck me down, and You alone will bind me up."

Those things (happenings) I thought would have utterly eaten me up with grief have now been placed at the feet of Jesus. The sorrow and grief expressed in the death and loss of my daughter and husband could have been the period or exclamation point that ended my hopes and dreams. But instead, a comma has been placed there and the word, but is inserted indicating that my life is not over. Danielle and Tom have transitioned from this earthly life to their eternal home, *but* Lydia shall live and not die. Lydia's horn, You shall exalt like the horn of a wild ox; Lydia shall be anointed with fresh oil... It is from His grace, by His Word and Spirit, that believers like me receive all the virtue and strength that keep us alive.

I know that I have often repeated in my discourse with family, friends, saints from other churches, and in my first book these words from Psalm 27:13: “I had, fainted unless I had believed to see the goodness of the Lord in the land of the living. (NKJV) That is my story; that is my testimony for the rest of my life! If death holds us down and keeps us from striving to move forward, keeps us in a continual state of foreboding and helplessness, snatches our faith away and renders it obsolete and of no effect, then the devil has won! He beat Jesus at the cross!

But my Bible tells me just the opposite. We serve a conquering Savior. He defeated death, hell, and the grave for us. We have the victory through Christ Jesus. His death, the sacrificial blood He shed for all of us is the guarantee for all of our burdens, trials, sicknesses, perplexities and perils.

Psalm 71:20-21 ESV says, “You who have made me see many troubles and calamities will revive me again; from the depths of the earth you will bring me up again. You will increase my greatness and comfort me again.”

Jesus and the disciples went to Bethany to see Mary and Martha after Lazarus died. They were very distraught and a bit angry that Jesus did not arrive before Lazarus died. They believed Jesus was the Son of God; they trusted him and were his personal friends.

> *When Martha said, "If you'd been here, my brother would not have died."* [23] *"Jesus said to her, "Your brother will rise again."*[24] *Martha answered, "I know he will rise again in the resurrection at the last day."*[25] *Jesus said to her, "I am the resurrection and the life. The one who believes in me will live, even though they die."*

Sometimes God has to make this book called *The Holy Bible* come alive and look us squarely in the face. As Christians, we live in denial the majority of the time. We do not believe in "the Suffering Savior" caricature of Jesus presented in the Book of Isaiah." We are like the Jews; we want a conquering king—a hero. We don't want any part of this suffering scenario. We figure that since we decided to make Jesus our choice, every day should be sunny, pleasant, without too much drama and sorrow. But that is not the true meaning of the cross as it relates to Jesus and his followers.

Thank God for deliverance, because I too lived at that address at one time. When we go through suffering we start believing that God owes us something, and it's not trouble! One of the definitions of salvation is deliverance.

Though it took a couple of years to see God's sovereignty and providential will in all that I had been through, I can now look back with awe, not regret, on how much God loved me, still loves me, and will continue to love me throughout life's inconsistencies.

I can truly say the safest place to be is in the arms of God. He never lets us down. He holds onto us and upholds us with His mighty hands. I'm living this life from eternity's point of view, but I want to experience the love, joy, hope and peace that serving the Lord promises before I die. There is a scripture in 1 Corinthians 2:9 which says," But as it is written: "Eye hath not seen, nor ear heard, neither have entered into the heart of man the things which God hath prepared for them that love Him

Another scripture speaks of the manifold blessing God wants to bequeath to us in Ephesians 3:20: Ephesians " Now unto him that is able to do exceeding abundantly above all that we ask or think, according to the power that worketh in us."

I don't know about you, but I would rather have the Lord's thinking, doing, working, and imagining at work in my life. I am going for the "BIG," because I serve a big God.

Getting through the transition was and is painful, but during this season in my life, things are beginning to settle down. I retired from the teaching profession in the summer of 2012. Currently, I am fulfilling my life's passion of preaching, teaching, mentoring, witnessing, and spreading the gospel. I am the founder and Senior Pastor of *Don't Forget to Say Your Prayers International Worship Center.* My son and his wife welcomed their second child in March of 2015. God's word says He will give you double for your trouble. The Ford name and legacy will carry on.

Additionally, my life has been enhanced by the entrance of a handsome male friend whom I just love spending time with. The blossoming of our friendship was God's idea not mine. It was definitely unexpected, but timely. After going through all of my objections to going out with a man, I finally dealt with my guilt, fears, and churchy high-mindedness. This step of the journey had to be God because I was concerned about what I believed people would say or think, thus, my reservations. I wrestled with that awhile and then reminded myself that I was the one who told my mentees, "You have to forget about what people think; get over it!" So, I followed my own advice and dismissed that objection; now we enjoy a great friendship.

Growing in the power and grace of God can be exciting if you embrace it. I've had a wonderful time during this restoration period. My life is more alive, productive, and enjoyable. I believe the best is yet to come. Fear robs you of the plans, and purpose God has for your life. He already had all these good, new surprises awaiting me on the other side of my trials and testing period. In the New Testament, several scriptures begin with the words, "*It came to pass.*" Those three words let us know troubles don't last always! There is an expiration date to your suffering. That is not to say it's the total end, but seasons do change and a time of refreshing helps us to breathe again and recover.

I'm not sure what people mean when they quote scriptures that infer you will or can take back what the devil has stolen from you. I know I will never see my daughter, husband, father and other loved ones again—at least not until I get to heaven. They have gone to be with the Lord. There is no replacement for your parents, children, or other loved ones when they die. The most we can do is change our attitude about death, losses, and other types of devastation and suffering. Some things can never be replaced. Again, it is our attitude that God is concerned about. Many of the storms in our lives that we complain, cry, and whine about aren't the same things God cries about. Much of our displeasure over suffering has to do with the loss of things that we idolize or have come to worship.

The Bible says to "Seek ye first the kingdom of heaven, and all these things will be added unto you" (Matthew 6:33). God is more interested in the eternal things of value, not the temporal things that we tend to prize. Faith, hope, and love are three things that have eternal consequences and value. They speak of cultivating relationships, valuing life, building an atmosphere of hope, and continuing to grow in our faith with God. Once these three things are gone, you have nothing of real value left.

At times our hope, faith, and love for God and people wax cold and get darkened by the ugliness that life brings. However, faith springs eternal because when we have given our lives to the Lord, and allow the Holy Spirit to abide within us. He is always there to illuminate the truth of His word to us. He gives us the refreshing we need to keep moving forward. God is the restorer of our salvation. The peace, joy, comforts, healing, and deliverance we have in Him creates a brand-new set of mercies each and every day.

My opportunities are raised exponentially because I passed the test! My expectancy is greater than it's ever been. I will bless the Lord and wait for Him to open doors that are cracked, but not quite open yet. I thank God for healing my emotions through the Holy Spirit. Anyone who comes into my life at this stage of the game is getting a softer, kinder person. If it had not been from the shaking, pressing, and beating, the oil could not flow. It took all of what I went through to prepare me for *greater*! My anointing was not the same yesterday as it is today, and neither my experience nor my education changed it. I'd rather have had an experience with God, lived through it, passed the test, and received a double portion of His grace and power than to have a few letters written in front or behind my name. Through it all, I learned to trust in Jesus; I learned to trust in God! Nothing shall ever separate me from the love of God. Because: Psalm 23 says:

"The Lord is my shepherd; I shall not want. [2] He maketh me to lie down in green [1] pastures: he leadeth me beside the still waters. [3] He restoreth my soul: he leadeth me in the paths of righteousness for his name's sake. [4] Yea, though I walk through the valley of the shadow of death, I will fear no evil: for thou art with me; thy rod and thy staff they comfort me. [5] Thou preparest a table before me in the presence of mine enemies: thou anointest my head with oil; my cup runneth over. [6] Surely goodness and mercy shall follow me all the days of my life: and I will dwell in the house of the Lord forever.

STORM CHASER

Don't forget to say your prayers, and thank God for restoration and healing.

He promises that He will take the good and the bad and work it out for our good. The Lord knows the way that we take, and when He has tried you and me, we shall come forth as pure gold. There are principles and processes that we must go through. However, we will not obtain the "Crown of Life" unless we persevere through all of our trials, temptations and disappointments. We must allow the Holy Spirit to empower us to reach beyond our present condition and circumstances to achieve the victory.

So when you feel confused beyond measure concerning your life and its misconceptions, when you have tried prayer, fasting, and numerous trips back and forth to the altar; when you have had the pastor, deacons, intercessors, and prophets pray, lay hands and anoint you with oil, only to discover the pain, heaviness, and dis-ease is still there—seek professional help. God has placed people in the body of Christ with the gifts of wisdom, knowledge, healing, and miracles. Take advantage of them and make full use of their ministry.

Below you will find several Scriptures which validate the worth, necessity, and rewards of passing the test. Yes, you will reap the benefits, favor and blessings of the Father.

Jeremiah 29:11 (KJV) *"For I know the plans I have for you," declares the Lord, "plans to prosper you and not to harm you, plans to give you hope and a future."*

Joel 2:25 (KJV) *"I will restore to you the years that the locust has eaten."*

Isaiah 61:7 (KJV) *"For your shame ye shall have double; and for confusion they shall rejoice in their portion: therefore in their land they shall possess the double: everlasting joy shall be unto them."*

Job 42:12 (KJV) *"So the LORD blessed the latter end of Job more than his beginning: for he had fourteen thousand sheep, and six thousand camels, and a thousand yoke of oxen, and a thousand she asses."*

Isaiah 61:3 (KJV)*"To appoint unto them that mourn in Zion, to give unto them beauty for ashes, the oil of joy for mourning, the garment of praise for the spirit of heavi-*

ness; that they might be called trees of righteousness, the planting of the LORD, that he might be glorified."

Deuteronomy 5:32–*33 (KJV) "So you shall observe to do just as the LORD your God has commanded you; you shall not turn aside to the right or to the left. You shall walk in all the way which the LORD your God has commanded you, that you may live and that it may be well with you, and that you may prolong your days in the land which you will possess."*

Hebrews 10:23 (KJV) *"Let us hold fast the confession of our hope without wavering, for He who promised is faithful."*

1 Peter 4:19 (KJV)*"Therefore, those also who suffer according to the will of God shall entrust their souls to a faithful Creator in doing what is right."*

Luke 9:62 (KJV)*"But Jesus said to him, 'No one, after putting his hand to the plow and looking back, is fit for the kingdom of God.'"*

STORM CHASING REFLECTIONS

(This space is provided for you to reflect on how you can apply what you've read)

ONE FINAL THOUGHT

Dear Reader,

Writing this second book has been both a labor of love and a testimony to the power of God in the life of a true believer. Without the Holy Spirit's power and work in my life, I would not have been able to survive the consecutive deaths of my loved ones, and the transition and transformation of my life in its current form. This venture has been a long journey. It took me two years to finish this second project. Going back through time and reliving the events of my pain and sorrow has been a difficult one. However, with each new day, with the light of the Lord shining brightly in my life, life has become less chaotic.

The title of the book reminded me of the gospel song, "Peace Be Still," which I learned and taught to members of a choir I use to play for in Schenectady, N.Y. The words, "Carest thou not that I perish," were so surreal to me while I was looking at my life's dreams being compassed about with huge, tumultuous waves, torrential downpours of rain, and boisterous thunderclaps above my head. I experienced the lyrics being played out in my life during Storm Alfred. It came upon the heels of Tom's death, followed by the car accident that could have ended my life, and left my only surviving child without both parents.

Through the pages of this book, I seek to help you, the reader, to hold on to God's unchanging hand. It is His hand that raises and quiets the storms in our lives. When He speaks the words, "Peace, be still," everything in our lives and in nature has to fall in line and take a back seat. This is a reminder to the faithfulness of God's enduring promises to watch over us and bring us out of the Jordan, onto dry land.

We must through many afflictions get to the other side of our Jordan. Many of us have *insurance* to pay for damaged property when the storms come and cause destruction, loss of property, flooding of houses and structures, etc.; what we need is some assurance that the God we serve will never leave us or forsake us—even in the midst of the storm. When our boat starts taking on water, when it gets filled to the brim, and becomes difficult to steer; when we have to make the difficult decision to abandon ship because the boards are breaking apart; God will throw us a lifeline. We might have to make it to shore on broken boards and pieces, but He promises that we *will* get to the other side.

Each chapter bared a piece of my soul as I journeyed back into time to excavate or pick up the pieces or residue that left marks and blemishes within my soul. This past Mother's Day, I went back to Schenectady to visit Danielle's grave site. It was my first visit back since the funeral in October of 2010. I had not been able to bring myself to go there because I was not ready to accept the closure I needed to move on with my life. A friend of mine, Wanda, met me and we made the journey there together. I picked up some flowers, and we found the location without too much difficulty. I knelt at her grave and read the marker, which I had not seen before. Prayers were said, tears were shed, but I could finally say goodnight to my baby girl, knowing that I would see her again on the other side.

At times, my heart gets a little heavy when I think of Tom and Danie not being here with me. But the Lord has blessed me three times with three such beautiful reminders of both my husband and my daughter. Their spirit lives in Jayla, Brianna, and Brittney. I pray this book will give you or somebody you know the resolve and faith to move from beyond the present moment of fear, loss, and hopelessness, to embrace the love of God, which He so graciously demonstrates through the loving leadership of Jesus Christ and the precious Holy Spirit. God Bless and, as always . . .

Don't forget to say your prayers!

PRAYER OF SALVATION

If you have read this book, I would like to offer you the best gift anyone could ever bestow upon you, and that is the free gift of salvation. It doesn't matter where you are currently in your life; it doesn't matter how many times you have messed up; it doesn't matter what your bloodline or whether you were born in the lap of luxury or born on the wrong side of the railroad tracks. The fact of the matter is God loves you!

God loves you—no matter who you are and no matter the experiences in your past. He loves you so much that He gave the most expensive gift that He had. He gave His only begotten Son for you. The Bible tells us that "Whoever believes in Him shall not perish but have eternal life" (John 3:16 NIV). Jesus, the Son of God laid down his life, died on the cross, and rose again so that we could spend eternity with Him in heaven. Not only that, but He gives us the power to live our best life here on earth. If you would like to receive Jesus into your life today, it is so simple. Say the following prayer out loud and mean it from your heart.

Heavenly Father, I come to You admitting that I am a sinner. Right now, I choose to turn away from my sin, and I ask You to cleanse me from all of my sins and unrighteousness. I believe that Your Son, Jesus, died on the cross to take away all my sins. I also believe that He rose again from the dead so that I might be forgiven of my sins and be made righteous through faith in Him. I call upon the name of Jesus Christ to be Savior and Lord of my life. Jesus, I choose to follow and obey You. I ask that You fill me with the power of the Holy Spirit. I declare that right now I am a child of God. I am free from sin and full of the righteousness of God. I am saved in Jesus's name. Amen.

If you prayed that prayer to receive Jesus Christ as your Savior for the first time, please contact us at:

Don't Forget to Say Your Prayers, Inc.
Reverend Lydia P. Ford
3 Andrea Lane
Bloomfield, CT 06002
www.dontforgettosayyourprayers.com

ABOUT THE AUTHOR

Reverend Lydia P. Ford, a licensed and ordained minister of the Gospel, is a gifted preacher, teacher, prayer warrior and seminar facilitator. She earned her undergraduate and graduate degrees in education from S.U.N.Y. at Cobleskill, S.U.N.Y. at Oneonta and S.U.N.Y. at Albany, respectively, and has taught elementary school for over 30 years. She received the coveted Apple for the Teacher Award, presented by the Iota Phi Lambda Sorority, Inc. Beta Chapter in November 2005 for excellence in teaching. An international minister, Rev. Ford traveled to the Bahamas in October of 2004, participating in the Connecticut State Missionary Congress of Christian Education Preaching Team. The team of preachers travels to the Bahamas and Barbados to spread the Gospel and provide monetary gifts and school supplies to several schools that they support.

Using her gifts of leadership, Rev. Ford has sponsored workshops, seminars, and has been a featured speaker at women's conference and retreats. Serving as Women's Ministry Director for over ten years, God richly blessed the ministry under her leadership. Rev. Ford completed the fall and spring, 2008 Pastoral Academy for Clinical Pastoral Training. She graduated from the Hartford Seminary's Black Ministers program and completed the "Faith Works" Faith Based Community Development Leadership Institute sponsored by the Capital Region Conference of Churches in May and June 2008 respectively. Most recently Rev. Ford was recognized by Cambridge Who's Who as VIP which qualified her for inclusion in the Cambridge Who's Who Registry of Executives, Professionals and Entrepreneurs 2010-2011 Edition.

In January of 2007, Rev. Ford founded an on-line prayer ministry, "Don't Forget To Say Your Prayers" which is an electronic resource where people all over the globe can learn how to pray effectively, give prayer requests, and expect God to work through this prayer ministry. Additionally, in April of 2009, Rev. Ford started Soul Talk, a mentorship ministry for and about women.

She is the founder and pastor of Don't Forget to Say Your Prayers International Worship Center. Rev. Ford lives in Connecticut and is the parent of an adult son, Trevor James Ford, a daughter-in-law Allyson, a son-in-law Jamus Geter and a doting nana to three beautiful granddaughters: Jayla Marie Geter, Brianna Marie Ford, and Brittany Renee Ford.

74445127R00113

Made in the USA
Columbia, SC
12 September 2019